The Casino Answer Book

How to Overcome the House Advantage when You Play Blackjack, Video Poker and Roulette

John Grochowski

Bonus Books, Inc.
Chicago, Illinois

02   01   00   99   98   5   4   3   2   1

Library of Congress Catalog Card Number 98-72459

ISBN 1-56625-107-9

Bonus Books, Inc.
160 E. Illinois St.
Chicago, IL 60611

Printed in the United States of America

Contents

Foreword

The book you're holding in your hand is a very important book. It's important the way a good review book is important for any professional—a doctor, lawyer, civil servant, teacher, police officer, firefighter, actuary—preparing to take the exam that demonstrates he or she knows the material and is competent to go out into the world and make money with it. What author John Grochowski (pronounced GROW-HOUSE-KEY) has done is compile a mountain of information on three of the most popular games in the casinos today—blackjack, video poker and roulette—to test the gambler's knowledge of the games he or she plays. If you have successfully mastered the information in this book, you are probably ready to take on the casinos with a much better than average chance of making some money at it. If you have not mastered your gambling material, this book will show you what things you have to do to increase the likelihood of coming home with a win. It will also point you in the direction of further study as any good review book does.

Still, a good review book not only questions you on the knowledge that you should have; it not only tells you when you're right or wrong, but it explains why a given answer is correct. John Grochowski has not merely written a good review book. He has written a great review book. Why? Because the explanations he gives for the correct answers are not only uniformly understandable, they are often enjoyable to read. Taking a dry subject such as gambling stats and strategies and making it into an enjoyable reading experience that is accessible to those of us who are not mathematicians is a great skill. Grochowski possesses that skill in spades . . . and hearts, and diamonds and clubs as well! You will find his insights and stories to be right on the money; his advice, razor sharp. You will find his writing style straightforward and pleasing. And as you devour the information in the upcoming chapters, you will say to yourself (as I said to myself): "Wow! This is one hell of a book!"

So who is John Grochowski? He's the new breed of gaming writer for one thing: schooled in the games; capable of understanding the diversity of gamblers' temperaments; able to write easily and coherently about topics that are often somewhat arcane and difficult; and a fellow who knows the industry from both sides of the table.

In the past, books about gambling, especially from major commercial publishers, were often written by individuals who had little real knowledge of what they were pontificating so authoritatively about. With some exceptions, the majority of gambling books were ill-informed and poorly written. The editors often decided on their gambling list thusly: "Hey, we need a gambling book for our fall list. Joe, doesn't your cousin go to the casinos and lose millions? Good, ask him if he can write up his ideas. Don't worry if he can't write, we'll get an editor to fix it up." The result was, of course, a book written by somebody who couldn't write edited by someone who didn't want to edit it. Quite often gambling books were written by gamblers with eccentric styles who basically told the reading public: "Look how great I am and look at what an idiot you are." These were anything but informative and helpful. Other gambling books would offer advice that was highly dubious. "Don't worry about the bets you make, just make sure your psychokinetic powers are working when you make them. " Thankfully, most of these books are no longer available or are entombed in card catalogues that never made their way onto computers.

Still there were some good books available in the past, even from commercial publishers—Edward O. Thorp's *Beat the Dealer* and Allan N. Wilson's *The Casino Gambler's Guide* are two that come readily to mind. But an expedition to your local bookstore was like panning for gold. You never knew what you were going to get when you opened the fly leaf of the book you bought.

Today is a somewhat different story.

At the top of the heap of today's gambling literature are excellent books written by mathematicians and computer experts that are often self-published. The overwhelming majority of these are ground-breaking books on blackjack. But the graphs, charts, indices, formulas and strategies contained in these books are daunting to the average person trying to get a handle on the games. I once had a reader write to me about another writer whom I admire and whose books I recommend highly: "I opened it and there were *dozens* of basic strategies to memorize. I said forget about it and closed the book. "

When you read John Grochowski you will not close the book and say: "Forget about it." Instead, you'll say: "This is terrific!" Grochowski has winnowed out the golden nuggets of important facts on blackjack, video poker, and roulette and made them into a pleasing chain of information that you can use to court Dame Fortune. He has sifted through all the information that is out there and given you the heart and soul of what you need to know to tackle today's games in today's casinos.

Although John Grochowski has a twice-weekly gaming column in *The Chicago Sun Times* and writes for many of the top magazines in the gaming field including *Midwest Gaming and Travel, Casino Executive,* and my own *The New Chance and Circumstance,* his early writing experiences had nothing to do with casinos or gambling. His career began in 1971 when he wandered into the sports department of the *Daily Illini,* the student newspaper of the University of Illinois. "They had advertised for sports writers. I liked sports so I decided to give it a shot. Eventually I became the sports editor and then chief copy editor and I have been at it ever since. "

When he graduated college, his first job was as a sports writer for *The Suburban Trib.* He then moved on to the *Colorado Spring Gazette-Telegraph* where he covered the Air Force football team and the Colorado Rockies hockey team (now the New Jersey Devils). In 1982 he joined the staff of *The Chicago Sun Times* where he worked as a copy editor in sports, news, features, business and commentary before landing the assignment in 1994 to write the "Gaming" column that has now made him a household name (however hard that name might be to pronounce) in the Midwest. In fact, Walter Thomason editor of *The Experts' Guide to Casino Games* (Carol Publishing) and the author of *The Ultimate Blackjack Book* (Carol Publishing) has dubbed Grochowski "Mr. Midwest Gaming." With the publication of this book, we might just have to drop the "Midwest" from this appellation!

Acknowledgments

This book would not have been possible without the infinite patience and understanding of my wife Marcy, the best sounding board for ideas that I know.

Thanks also to Frank Scoblete, who brought me together with Bonus Books.

And special thanks go to those who have so often provided me with information and support in the four years I've been writing gaming columns for the Chicago Sun-Times. The time they've spent with me was invaluable in compiling the answers here. They include, but are by no means limited to, Lenny Frome, Deke Castleman, Anthony Curtis, Howard Schwartz, Jean Scott, Al Sikirdji, Lorraine Nelson, Mary Phalen, Kathy Posner, Monica Kasley, Kathleen McLaughlin, Don Wren, Keenan Wright and many, many more.

Introduction

Ever wonder when, and why, blackjack rose to its overwhelming popularity among casino table games? Or why it's usually dealt from multiple decks of cards? Or why it should make a difference to the player how many decks are used anyway?

Ever wonder just how a video poker machine "decides" what cards you're going to be dealt? Or why there's so much video poker and so little video blackjack? Or whether video poker isn't really just a slot machine in disguise?

Ever wonder where the "French" game of roulette has its origins? Or how a flaw in the game allowed an engineer to break the bank at Monte Carlo? Or why the number of zeroes on a wheel makes a difference?

I want to know the best way to play this blackjack hand or that video poker hand, just as any educated player should. But I'm also intrigued by the backgrounds and fun facts behind the games. And when it comes to playing strategies, I want to know the whys as well as the whats. Why should I or shouldn't I insure a blackjack? Why should I or shouldn't I keep a Queen instead of a low pair in video poker?

Since 1994, I've been exploring questions like that with readers of my twice-weekly *Chicago Sun-Times* gambling column.

This book is arranged in 21 quizzes. There are multiple choice questions, definitions, true and false, even a couple of matching games. Many of the questions deal with playing strategy, but others will simply challenge your general knowledge of the games.

But more than a book of questions, this is a book of answers. Look up the answer to a multiple-choice question, and you'll find more than just A, B or C. The questions are jump-off points for mini-essays, excuses to go off on tangents and relate casino experiences and things I've learned while looking up other things.

In this book, you'll find answers to questions about blackjack, video poker and roulette—blackjack and video poker because they are games in which player decisions affect the outcome, roulette because it is one of our oldest games of chance and a favorite of systems players.

As for answers to questions about slot machines, craps, keno and more . . . those are subjects for another time.

Blackjack Hand Number 1: Getting Started

Whether we've played at the kitchen table or in the casino, most of us know the basics of blackjack. The game is also called "21," after its optimal hand. Cards from 2 through 10 count as their face value; Jacks, Queens and Kings each count as 10, and Aces may count as either 1 or 11.

The dealer gives two cards to each player and takes two for himself. The player then may "hit"—take another card—until he's either satisfied with his total or he "busts" with a total exceeding 21. If he busts, he loses. The dealer then plays out his hand until he either has a total of 17 or better or he busts. If he busts, he pays off all players with hands still alive. If he reaches 17 or better, he pays off players with higher totals of 21 or less.

The raw basics are easy, but how much do you know about the game behind the game—origins, trivia, etiquette and strategies? As we deal out our first hand of 21 multiple choice questions, see if you know these fun facts about blackjack.

1. The game of blackjack got its name from:

    A. Its inventor, "Black Jack" Callahan

    B. Special payoffs in early games

    C. Black Jack's Saloon in turn-of-the-century Tombstone, Arizona.

2. Blackjack's roots are in:

    A. Native American games

1

B. Asia

C. Europe

3. Other names for the game of blackjack include:

A. Pontoon

B. Van John

C. Bust-out

4. Among all casino games in the United States, blackjack's popularity ranks behind only:

A. Slot machines

B. Craps

C. Video poker

5. Among table games in the United States, blackjack accounts for:

A. 20 percent of casino revenue

B. 35 percent of casino revenue

C. 50 percent of casino revenue

6. Blackjack's popularity rose to its current level among table games:

A. In the 1940s

B. In the 1960s

C. In the 1980s

7. Blackjack's popularity gains were sparked by:

A. Streamlined rules that were more favorable to the player

B. Glamour from association with entertainment's "Rat Pack"

C. Publication of *Beat the Dealer*

8. Blackjack usually is played at a table with seats for:

A Seven players

B. Six players

C. Five players

9. **The house estimates players will lose an average of:**

   A. $2 for every $100 bet
   B. $10 for every $100 bet
   C. $50 for every $100 bet

10. **Compared with other casino games, the house advantage on blackjack is:**

    A. Larger
    B. Smaller
    C. About the same

11. **The house has an advantage in blackjack because:**

    A. Dealer's rules for hitting and standing favor the house
    B. The player finishes his hand before the dealer
    C. Player options are designed to give the house an edge

12. **The seat all the way to the players' right is called:**

    A. First base
    B. The anchor
    C. The starter

13. **A player may bet:**

    A. Only on his own hand
    B. On other players' hands
    C. On the dealer's hand

14. **Compared with blackjack in the 1950s, today's game is:**

    A. More standardized
    B. More varied
    C. About the same

15. **Compared with blackjack in the 1950s, today's game:**

    A. Gives the house a bigger advantage
    B. Give the player a better run for his money
    C. Is about the same

16. Players let the dealer know whether they want another card by:

    A. Calling out "hit" or "stand"

    B. Scratching the table with their cards

    C. Signalling with their hands, without touching their cards

17. A color-coded placard on the table tells players:

    A. The minimum and maximum bets allowed at the table

    B. House rules for the game

    C. The dealer's name

18. Video blackjack usually is worse than the table game for the player because:

    A. The cards are not random

    B. The player doesn't know how many decks are in use

    C. Blackjacks pay only even money

19. Modern basic strategy was developed:

    A. In France, in the early 1900s

    B. By a team of U.S. Army mathematicians in the 1950s

    C. By a 12-year-old boy on a home computer in the 1980s

20. It is possible to gain an edge in the game of blackjack

    A. By counting cards

    B. By using a betting progression

    C. Never

21. If the house spots a player good enough to have an edge, it may:

    A. Bar him from playing

    B. Limit the size of his bets

    C. Shuffle more frequently

Blackjack Hand Number 1: Getting Started Answers

1. B. The game of 21 played in illegal casinos in the early 1900s sometimes paid a bonus if a two-card 21 was made up of an Ace of spades and a Jack of spades. Others paid extra for an Ace of spades combined with a Jack of either spades or clubs. In either case, the black Jack was the key, and to players, blackjack was the name of the game.

Today, the payoff on a two-card 21 has been standardized at 3-2. Place a $5 bet in Atlantic City, Las Vegas, Tunica County in Mississippi, or Joliet in Illinois, and if you win with a two-card total of 21 you'll be paid $7.50. It doesn't matter if the Jack is black, or if there's a Jack at all. An Ace of hearts combined with a 10 of diamonds or any other two-card 21 will get you the 3-2 payoff.

There are sometimes exceptions. I've seen casinos that increase the payoff to 2-1 instead of 3-2 if the two-card 21 consists of an Ace and Jack of spades—a $5 pet pays $10 instead of $7.50. Others use other bonus combinations—for a time, the Dixie Duck cruising off Key West, Florida, was offering 2-1 on an Ace of diamonds combined with a Jack of diamonds.

How much difference does such a bonus make? There are 64 possible two-card 21s in a single 52-card deck. Singling out one of those 64 combinations to pay out 2-1 instead of 3-2 gives the player an average of an extra 3.6 cents per $100 wagered—a 0.036 percent gain, if you're keeping score. Nothing to hop a plane for, but if you're in the neighborhood, why not take advantage of a little something extra?

2. C. Origins are in Europe, though exactly where is uncertain. Enthusisasts in France, Spain and Italy all claim their nation gave rise to blackjack. The French Vingt-Un, the Spanish Uno y Trente and the Italian baccarat all have similiarities. Interestingly, a new game called Super 7½ has made its way onto a few casino floors in the United States. The game has similarities to blackjack, and also closely resembles a much older Italian game called 7½. It's possible that the development of Super 7½ in the 1990s has given us a clue to the beginnings of blackjack.

3. A and B. Pontoon and Van John both arose in the South as nicknames for blackjack, probably centered around the illegal New Orleans casinos that were among the most lavish in the country in the 1940s and '50s. Both names appear to be a corruption of the French name Vingt-Un.

4. A. Hands down, slot machines are the most popular casino game in the U.S. Second place is a close call between blackjack and video poker. As we approach the new millennium, all electronic gaming devices—slots, video poker, video keno, video blackjack and others—account for about 70 percent of casino revenue. Video poker is roughly 20 percent of the electronic gaming market, or about 14 percent of overall casino revenues. Blackjack, by far the most popular of all casino table games, accounts for about 15 percent of casino revenue.

There are regional differences. In Nevada, where video poker has a very strong local base of players, video poker actually ranks number 2 behind slots, ahead of blackjack. In newer gaming markets, blackjack has a wider than average lead over video poker.

5. C. About half of all casino revenue from table games comes from blackjack.

That led me to an interesting exchange with another gambling writer a few years ago. We were chatting on the phone about a gaming expo at which we'd both be giving seminars.

"Do you play blackjack?" he asked.

"Sure do," I replied. "Are you going to play while you're in town?"

"Not me. Blackjack's the worst game in the house."

"Excuse me?"

"That's where they make all their money. My friend who runs a casino in Las Vegas asks me, 'Why do you think we put blackjack tables right up front? That's our biggest money-maker.'"

I was being tested. Blackjack is a big money-maker for the casinos, but that's mostly because so many people play it. The volume of wagers on blackjack dwarfs those on other table games. Casino revenue follows along.

6. B. Blackjack rose to preeminence among table games in the 1960s. Earlier, the dominant table game at American casinos had been craps.

Craps was the serviceman's game of the World War II generation. From games behind the barracks all the way to the foxholes, soldiers took dice to war. When they came home and started visiting Las Vegas and Reno, craps was the game they wanted to play. That lasted into the early '60s, when craps' popularity was overtaken by blackjack. The gap has been widening ever since, and continues to widen as blackjack holds onto its popularity and craps' popularity declines with the war generation in late life. Today craps remains the number two table game, but in a secondary role, with perhaps 20 percent of the table games market compared with 50 percent for blackjack.

7. C. Edward O. Thorp's best-selling *Beat the Dealer*, first published in 1962, caused a sensation. Thorp was the first to publish a system for counting cards to gain an edge over the casino. The message players took from Thorp's book and the publicity surrounding it was, "Blackjack can be beaten." Never mind that most players lack the knowledge, discipline or bankroll to actually beat the game, they knew deep down that it was a game that could be beaten. If a gambler knows there's a game that can be beaten, the natural response is to try to beat it. By the end of the '60s, blackjack had overtaken craps as the most popular casino game, and it hasn't been challenged since.

8. A. The standard blackjack table has seven seats and seven betting spots, although there are variations.

A few years ago, to get an inside view of casino operations, I enrolled as a student at the week-long William F. Harrah Institute of Casino Entertainment. The institute was a crash course in all things casino, from the surveillance room to the count rooms, from the games themselves to marketing the casino. There were speakers from both inside and outside the Harrah's organization to give a well-balanced view of how casinos work.

At one of the sessions, it was pointed out to us that Harrah's Las Vegas uses five-seat tables. The reason is that with fewer players, it takes less time to complete a blackjack hand. More hands are played per hour and the casino makes a bigger profit per seat. The tables are smaller, so the casino can put more tables in the same space and get about the same number of seats as if standard-sized tables were installed. Just by using a different piece of furniture, the casino makes more money.

Interestingly, Harrah's customers liked the new tables. They didn't feel as crowded. So a decision Harrah's made on the basis of potential revenue was also seen as a customer-service touch by its guests.

On the other end, Empress Casino in Joliet, Illinois, has some tables with seven seats but eight betting spots. That enables a player who wishes to play two hands at once to do so without preventing a full complement of players from sitting at the table. That also has as a customer service benefit, since the eight-spotters are slightly larger than the usual seven-seat, seven-spot tables.

9. A. The house assumes the average player will lose about $2 to $2.50 for each $100 wagered. That's not as good as a basic strategy player will do, but it's still better than the average outcome on roulette, Caribbean Stud or the slots.

Casinos use that average in rating players for comps—complimentary casino meals, discounted rooms and more. If you play one hour of blackjack, betting $10 per hand at 50 hands per hour, you risk $500. On that basis, the casino figures a theoretical win—their math says that in the long run, guests playing at that level will lose an average of $10 per hour. If you have your play rated, the casino uses that figure to offer you comps. It's not going to give you back the full $10 per hour in meals or room discounts, but it will kick back a percentage of that theoretical win—anywhere from 10 percent to 40 percent of it depending on the casino and competitive conditions—in the form of casino comps.

In determining your comp status, the theoretical win is more important than your actual wins and losses. You might lose $100 in an hour instead of $10, but your hosts know that if you play very often, that will be offset by some winning sessions and others in which you lose less than expected. An experienced player will expect to be comped when he's winning as well as when he's losing. To make that fiscally feasible, the casino can't comp merely on the basis of the occasional larger-than-expected loss.

10. B. The house has a smaller edge on blackjack than on almost any casino game, provided the player is knowledgeable. A player who mimics the dealer—always hitting 16 and under, always standing on 17 and over, regardless of what the dealer has—gives the house an edge of about 5.7 percent. What that means is that the player loses an average of $5.70 per $100 wagered.

But a player who takes the time to learn basic strategy can cut that house edge all the way to 0.5 percent—a little more or less, depending on house rules. The player now loses an average of only 50 cents per $100 played. (Basic strategy is detailed in any good book on blackjack and most good general gaming guides. Frank Scoblete's *Best Blackjack* has a section on basic strategy, and my own *Gaming: Cruising the Casinos With Syndicated Gambling Columnist John Grochowski,* includes several columns I've written on basic strategy). And those who take it to the next level and learn to count cards can even gain a slight edge.

Given that the vast majority won't become card counters, how does a basic strategy player's average 50-cent loss per $100 played compare with other casino games? A craps player loses $1.41 per $100 on the pass line or $1.40 per $100 on don't pass, but there's a wide variety of worse bets. The one-roll proposition on 7, for example, will cost you $16.67 per $100 wagered. In baccarat, you'll lose $1.17 per $100 on banker or $1.36 per $100 on player. At an American double-zero roulette wheel, almost all wagers will cost you $5.26 per $100. The exception is the five-number bet on 0, 00, 1, 2 and 3, which costs $7.89 per $100. That's right in line with Caribbean Stud, at about $5.22 per $100 in antes.

Slots? That depends on the region. In downtown Las Vegas, with the highest slot paybacks in the country, the casino takes about $5 per $100 wagered on quarter slots and a little more than $4 per $100 on dollar slots. In Indiana, with less competitive pressure, the casino keeps about $8 per $100 on quarter slots and $6 per $100 on dollar slots. Some video poker machines offer slightly better than 100 percent payback with expert play, but such machines are rare outside Nevada.

Overall, blackjack gives the educated player one of his best shots to win. A player who doesn't want to take the time to learn to play blackjack well will do better at craps (if he sticks to pass and don't pass) or baccarat.

11. B. The house's only advantage in blackjack is that the player has a chance to go bust first. If both the player and dealer bust on the same hand, the house wins.

If the player uses the same hit/stand strategy as the dealer, the player will bust 28 percent of the time, and the dealer also will bust 28 percent of the time. The house edge is the intersection of those two bust percentages—the 28 percent of 28 percent of the time that both player and dealer bust. That's about 8 percent of all hands. If there were no compensating rules, the house would have about an 8 percent edge and would win about $8 per $100 wagered.

There are compensating rules and ways to trim that house

edge, of course. See *Blackjack Hand Number 4: Good Rules, Bad Rules.*

12. A. The seat all the way to the players' right is first base, and the first baseman is the first player to receive cards and play out his hand.

Conversely, the player all the way to the players' left is the third baseman, or the anchor. If you're a new player and don't want heat from others at the table, avoid sitting at third base. Many players mistakenly believe that the third baseman has an effect on the whole table way out of proportion to the importance of one hand. If they believe the third baseman has made a mistake, some players will get angry, make snide remarks or even scream at him.

Even if they recognize that the third baseman has made the right play for himself, some players get huffy if they think his play has been bad for the table. A friend of mine asked me one day if he'd made a mistake by hitting a 12 when the dealer showed a 2 as his face-up card. As it happens, this is a good play, a basic strategy fine point that the majority of players miss. It didn't work this time—my friend drew a 10 and busted with 22 and the dealer, with a Queen face down, drew a 9 for 21—but it's still the correct play.

"But when I did it, this man and a woman started yelling at me that I'd taken the dealer's bust card," he said. "They said at third base I had to play for the table, and if I was going to play like that they were going to leave."

My friend stood his ground, and his tormentors stomped off.

It's all nonsense, of course. Blackjack is not a team sport. No one is going to reimburse you if you make a poor percentage play for the sake of the other players. And no one really knows what order the cards are coming out anyway. If the order of the 9 and the 10 had been reversed, my friend would have been saving the table by taking a hit.

Just that happened to me at the Tropicana in Las Vegas one night—and this time someone actually noticed. Same situation: I had 12, the dealer showed a 2. I hit a 9 for my 21, the dealer turned up a 10, then drew a King to bust and the whole table won. From the other end of the table came a cheer: "Great stop! What a third baseman!"

Nice when it works that way.

13. A. At most American tables, the player may bet only on his own hand. That's not the case overseas. In many foreign casinos, bettors gather behind those seated at the table and pick a hand on which to bet. Often, the custom is that the player seated defers hit/stand decisions to the player with the biggest bet on the hand.

Not my favorite way to play. I'd just as soon be responsible for my own hand, thanks.

14. B. Today's game offers a wide variety of optional rules. The standard Las Vegas Strip game of the 1950s—single-deck, player may double down on any first two cards, player may split any pair, dealer stands on all 17s—has all but disappeared. Today there are one, two, four, six, and eight deck games. One casino might allow the player to double down only on 9, 10 and 11 while the joint next door allows double downs on split pairs and lets the player surrender half his bet instead of playing out a bad hand.

It's a mix-and-match world. Which rules help and which hinder the player? See *Blackjack Hand Number 4: Good Rules, Bad Rules.*

15. A. For the most part, the house has a bigger edge in today's game than it would have if we were playing 1950s rules. The old Las Vegas Strip rules on a single-deck game yield an even game—actually, a basic strategy player has a 0.01 percent edge on the house. When those Strip rules were common, there weren't any basic strategy players, so the house wasn't losing any money on the game. After *Beat the Dealer* scared casinos in the early 1960s, multiple-deck games became common and rules were tightened to scare off card counters. The rules have been relaxed over the years, but the multiple decks have stayed. Usually, today's single-deck games have tighter rules than in the old days, and multiple-deck games offer more player options.

16. B or C, depending on whether cards are dealt face up or face down. In most single-deck and double-deck games, cards are dealt face down. The player picks them up in one hand—the casino is wary of cheating and you'll get a warning from the dealer if you use two hands. When it's your turn, you signal you want another card by scratching the cards on the table. If you want to stand, you slide the cards under the chips on your betting spot.

If the cards are dealt face up, indicate hit or stand with a hand motion. To stand, flatten your palm and hold it over the cards. To hit, use a hand motion toward yourself, or point at the cards or the table next to the cards.

Never touch your cards in a game dealt face up. Nowadays you'll just get a polite request not to touch them the first time or two. When face-up games first became common in the '60s, sterner measures were taken from the first offense. Common casino policy was that if the customer touches the cards, the dealer slaps his hand. No more. The expansion of gaming options has meant casinos have had to deal with more new players and make extra effort to keep their guests. It's a more player-friendly atmosphere than it used to be. Still, if you repeatedly touch the cards when you're not supposed to, you're begging to be asked to leave the table.

17. A and B. There are some variations from casino to casino, but usually a red placard means there is a $5 minimum bet at that table, a green placard means a $25 minimum and black means a $100 minimum. That corresponds to the normal colors of casino chips: red for $5, green for $25 and black for $100.

Some, but not all, house rules also may be listed on the placard. I recently encountered a sign that said: "BLACKJACK. $5 minimum. $500 maximum. Split any pair except Aces three times (4 hands). One card on split Aces." That told me a lot about the game. I knew before sitting down that I had to bet at least $5 and couldn't bet any more than $500 on a hand. If I was dealt two cards of the same denomination, I could split and make each card the start of a separate hand. If I received the same denomination again, I could resplit again, and again until I had a total of four hands. However, if I had a pair of Aces, I could split only once and receive only one more card on each Ace.

I couldn't tell just by looking, however, if I could double down after splitting a pair, or if I could surrender. That I had to ask the dealer. And that's what you should do. If you have a question about house rules, ask the dealer.

18. C. Most video blackjack machines pay even money on two-card 21s instead of the 3-2 paid on the tables. On video blackjack machines that do pay 3-2 on blackjack, the player should be sure to play an even number of coins. If you play two quarters and are dealt a blackjack, you'll get three quarters in winnings. But if you play only one quarter, which at 3-2 would pay 37.5 cents, you'll be stuck with only one quarter in winnings. The machine doesn't have any 12 ½-cent pieces to make up the difference.

19. B. The Army team of Baldwin, Cantey, Maisel and McDermott published their basic strategy in 1956 in the *Journal of the American Statistical Association.* There were refinements in the next several years, notably from Julian Braun's computer studies at IBM in Chicago. Refinements are still made whenever a casino tries a new rules variation, but essentially the best strategy for playing your cards has remained intact since the early 1960s.

20. A. Card counters can gain a small edge. Unlike most casino games, the odds change constantly in blackjack. Each card dealt out and no longer available changes the balance between player and dealer. Card counters learn to identify when that balance swings in favor of the player. Then they increase their bets. See *Blackjack Hand Number 9: Keeping count.*

21. A, B and C are all measures that have been used to deter card counters. Not all states can bar counters from playing, however. While in Nevada the courts have held that casinos are private clubs and may bar anyone from playing for any reason, other states are more restrictive. In Illinois, for example, each casino must submit a list of internal controls on every game to the Illinois Gaming Board. The Illinois Gaming Board has never approved a set of internal controls that would allow a casino to bar card counters. Shuffling early or limiting bet size is another matter—those are allowed.

Blackjack Hand Number 2: Definitions

Every casino game has its own jargon. Most of it's easy—anyone who's played blackjack knows "hit" and "stand." Some of it's more obscure. I get letters from readers nearly every week asking, "What's insurance? What's surrender?"

Do you know? Then define the following:

1. Hit
2. Stand
3. Blackjack
4. Bust
5. Push
6. Up card
7. Face-up game
8. Pitch
9. Shoe
10. Cut card
11. Soft hand
12. Hard hand
13. Dealer's rules
14. Double down
15. Split pairs
16. Resplit
17. Double after split
18. Insurance
19. Even money
20. Surrender
21. Basic strategy

Blackjack Hand Number 2: Definitions Answers

1. To hit is to take another card.

2. To stand is to refuse any more cards.

3. Besides being the name of the game, a blackjack is a two-card 21. That's an Ace along with a 10, Jack, Queen or King. If the player is dealt a blackjack, he's paid 3-2, unless the dealer has one too. Let's say the player has a $5 bet on the table and he's dealt an Ace and a King. If the dealer does not have a blackjack, the player wins $7.50. However, if the dealer also has a two-card 21, it's a tie and the player just keeps his original wager.

4. To bust is to draw cards that give the hand a total value of more than 21. For the player, busting is an automatic loser—it doesn't matter what the dealer has. A dealer who busts loses only to players who stand without busting.

5. A push is a tie. If you have 18 and the dealer has 18, you push and no money changes hands.

6. The dealer's first two cards are dealt with one face down and the other face up. The one dealt face up is the up card. The one dealt face down is the down card or hole card.

7. A face-up game is one in which all players' cards are dealt face up. That's typical in games with four or more decks. Usually, in single-deck and double-deck blackjack, players' cards are dealt face down, and the player may pick them up. In a face-up game, the players may not touch the cards.

8. Pitch is the method of dealing in a single-deck or double-deck game in which the dealer holds the cards in his hand. While holding the cards in one hand, the dealer uses his other hand to take the top card off the deck and pitch it across the table to the player.

9. A shoe is a rectangular box, usually made of plastic, used to hold the cards in a game using multiple decks. After shuffling, the dealer places the cards in the shoe. To deal, he slides them, one card at a time, out of an opening in the front.

The most common shoe games use four, six or eight decks, but in some gaming jurisdictions, all blackjack games are required to be dealt from a shoe. When you encounter a single-deck or double-deck game in Nevada, there will be no shoe. After shuffling, the dealer will hold the cards in one hand, then deal with the other. In Illinois, on the other hand, there are no single-deck games and the rare double-deck games must be dealt from a shoe.

That can have some unintended consequences, as one Illinois casino found out. Nearly all shoe games are dealt with all players' cards face up. That's, in part, a security measure. Players may not touch the cards in a face-up game, making it more difficult to cheat by substituting cards. (The casino already does everything in its power to stop such shenanigans by monitoring games from its surveillance room.) But dealing cards face-up in a two-deck game also is an enormous help to card counters, who track the cards played in order to identify favorable situations. When those situations occur, they increase their bets.

Empress Casino in Joliet, Illinois, briefly tried offering a double-deck game with the same rules as their six-deck and eight-deck games. The two-decker was dealt from a shoe, with all players' cards face up. It was a counter's dream, and the game quickly disappeared.

10. The cut card is a colored plastic card used by a player to, interestingly enough, cut the cards. After the dealer shuffles, he gives the cut card to a player. The dealer holds the cards, and the player slides in the cut card. All cards in front of the cut card are then moved to the back.

In most casinos, the cut card also is used to indicated a shuffle point. After the player has cut and the front cards have been moved to the back, the dealer takes the plastic card and places it in the deck. As cards are being dealt, when the cut card comes out the dealer finishes the hand in progress, then shuffles before the next hand.

Different casinos place the shuffle card at different points. It's rare to see more than half the cards dealt in a single-deck game, but there can be a wide variation in shuffle points in multiple-deck games. In a six-deck game, I've seen anywhere from one-half deck to two-and-one-half decks cut out of play. That's largely an indication of how much the casino fears card counters. The more cards that are dealt, the more accurate a count can be kept.

11. A soft hand is one in which an Ace is being used as an 11 and which can't be busted by taking just one more card. Ace-6, for example, is a soft 17. Add an 11 for the Ace to the 6, and you have a 17. However, the hand also could be counted as 7-1 for the Ace plus the 6. That makes the total soft. If the player hits that soft 17 and draws a 5, he does not bust with 22. Instead, he counts the Ace as 1 and has 12. Then he makes another decision as to whether to hit or stand.

12. A hard hand is just the opposite of a soft hand: there is no Ace being used as an 11 that can become a 1 if necessary. Remember our soft 17 from the previous answer, an Ace and a 6? If we draw a 5 to that, we now have a hard 12: an Ace counted as one, plus a 6, plus a 5.

Hard hands of 12 and more can be busted with just one hit. In our example of the soft 17 that turned into a hard 12 by drawing a 5, we bust if we hit and are dealt a 10, Jack, Queen or King. Any of those cards take our total to 22, and we lose.

13. Dealers' rules determine whether the dealer hits or stands on any hand. Those rules are printed clearly on the table felt. The felt will say either "Dealer must draw to 16 and stand on all 17s," or "Dealer must hit soft 17." At any table, the dealer hits any hand totaling 16 or less. At some tables, he stands on any 17, hard or soft, whether it consists of 9-8, Ace-3-3 or any other combination. At others, he hits soft 17: the dealer stands on 10-7 or 6-6-5 or any other hard 17, but hits Ace-6, Ace-Ace-5 or any other soft 17.

Soft 17s can have more than two cards. A reader of my newspaper column once called to complain because he thought the dealer hit when he shouldn't have. At a casino where the dealer hit soft 17s, my reader stood on an 18. The dealer started with a 2 and a 3, drew an Ace, then another Ace for 17. He hit again, then drew a 3 to total 20. My reader, who stood with a total of 18, thought only Ace-6 was soft 17, that having 17 with four cards meant the dealer should stand. That would have made his 18 a winner. That's not the way it works. Ace-Ace-2-3 is soft 17. So is Ace-Ace-5, Ace-Ace-Ace-2-2, even Ace-Ace-Ace-Ace-Ace-Ace-Ace.

14. After receiving his first two cards, the player may double down by placing a second bet equal to his original wager. In exchange for being allowed to double his bet, the player is limited to drawing just one more card.

Doubling down enables the player to maximize his potential profit in situations that favor the player. The trick is to recognize those favorable situations.

15. When the player's hand starts with two cards of the same denomination, the player may split the pair and use each card as the starting point for a separate hand. For example, if the hand starts with two 8s, the player may split by placing a second wager equal to his first. Each 8 then becomes the first card in a new hand. Just as with doubling down, splitting pairs is a great option for the player, provided he uses it wisely.

16. Most casinos allow the player to resplit pairs. If the player splits a pair of 8s and receives yet another 8 as the second card in one of his resulting hands, he may split again. That would leave him with three hands, each starting with an 8. Usually, the casino limits the player to two splits for a total of three hands or three splits for a total of four hands. A few, notably the Las Vegas

Club in downtown Las Vegas, allow unlimited resplits, and some allow pairs to be split only once in a hand.

17. Double after split means the casino allows the player to double down after splitting pairs. If the player splits 8s then draws a 3 as the second card in one hand, he has an 11. Some casinos will then allow him to double down on the basis of that two-card total.

18. Insurance is an option made available to players whenever the dealer has an Ace face-up as one of his first two cards. It essentially is a side bet that the dealer has a blackjack. The player who takes insurance places a wager half the size of his original bet. If the dealer then has a 10-value card—a 10, Jack, Queen or King—face down to complete a blackjack, the insurance bet is paid at 2-1.

What that means is that the player who loses his regular bet breaks even for the hand. Let's say you've bet $10, your first two cards total 20 and the dealer has an Ace face-up. If you decide to take insurance, you bet another $5. The dealer checks his hole card. If he has a blackjack, he turns his hole card face up. You lose your original $10 bet, but your $5 insurance bet wins and is paid at 2-1. That gives you $10 in insurance winnings, balancing out the $10 loss on your regular bet and leaving you back where you started.

Is this a good bet? We'll take a look at that in *Blackjack Hand Number 4: Good Rules, Bad Rules.*

19. Even money comes into play when the player has a blackjack and the dealer has an Ace face-up. If the player takes insurance, he guarantees that he wins an amount equal to his original bet. The outcome is the same regardless of whether the dealer has blackjack, so most casinos will allow the player to simply call out, "even money," rather than requiring him to go through the motions of placing a bet half the size of his original wager.

To see how this works, let's use the same setup as in the previous answer. The player bets $10, is dealt a blackjack and the dealer has an Ace face-up. If the player decides to take insurance, he makes a $5 insurance wager. Then, if the dealer has blackjack, the player pushes on his blackjack bet, but wins $10 for his 2-1 payoff on insurance for a profit of $10 on the hand—a profit equal to his original bet. If the dealer does not have blackjack, the player loses his $5 insurance wager, but wins $15 for the 3-2 payoff on his blackjack, also leaving a net profit of $10.

If the player does not take insurance in this situation, he could wind up with a larger profit because that $15 win if the dealer doesn't have blackjack isn't diluted by an insurance wager. The downside is that he could wind up with no profit at all: if the dealer has blackjack and the player hasn't insured, the result is just a push.

Is even money a good bet? Shuffle that through your mind until we get to *Blackjack Hand Number 4: Good Rules, Bad Rules.*

20. Surrender is a player option that seemed to be all but dead a few years ago, but has made a big comeback in Nevada. Instead of playing out the hand, a player who does not like his first two cards may surrender half his bet. If the player may surrender regardless of whether the dealer has blackjack, it's called "early surrender," a very rare option offered briefly in 1997 by the Holiday Inn Boardwalk on the Las Vegas Strip. If the player must wait until the dealer checks to see if he has blackjack, it's called "late surrender." It's in the late surrender format that this option has had its resurgence in the latter part of the '90s.

21. Basic strategy is the method by which players in the know make their decisions on whether to hit or stand, split or double down. Players who count cards tinker with basic strategy; an imbalance in the proportion of high cards and low cards remaining to be played can make adjustments in play profitable.

For the vast majority of players who are not card counters, however, there is one best play for each player's hand taken in conjunction with the dealer's up card. To give a hint of things to come, let's say the player has a hard 16. If the dealer has a 6 face up, basic strategy says the player should stand. If the dealer has a 7 up, the player should hit.

Anyone who's going to play blackjack should learn basic strategy. Any good blackjack book or general gaming guide includes a basic strategy discussion.

Blackjack Hand Number 3: True or False Questions

Things that people believe about blackjack don't always mesh with reality. Try to sort out which of the following statements are fact and which are fiction:

1. **A 6 is a bust card. If the dealer has one face up, he's more likely than not to go over 21.**

   True
   False

2. **The player should always insure a blackjack. It's the only "sure thing" in the casino.**

   True
   False

3. **Blackjack can be beaten.**

   True
   False

4. **The player is just as likely as the dealer to get a blackjack.**

   True
   False

5. **When deciding whether to hit or stand, the player should always assume the dealer has a 10 face down and will get a 10 on his next card.**

True
False

6. **12s are 10-magnets. A player who hits 12 busts more often than not.**

   True
   False

7. **For the dealer, a 2 is a great card, as good as an Ace for the player.**

   True
   False

8. **The player should always split pairs of Aces or 8s.**

   True
   False

9. **Players who tip the dealer get better cards.**

   True
   False

10. **Counting cards is illegal. Card counters can be prosecuted on felony fraud charges.**

    True
    False

Blackjack Hand Number 3: True or False Answers

1. False. Strictly speaking, there are no dealer "bust cards," only cards with which he busts a little more often than others.

On every possible face-up card, the dealer actually will make 17 or better more than 50 percent of the time. Even with a 6 face up, the dealer will bust only about 42 percent of the time. And most players don't realize that the dealer actually busts most often with a 5 face up—about 43 percent of the time.

It's a common cause of frustation for blackjack players. There are streaks when the dealer seems to make his hand every time he shows a 2, 3, 4, 5 or 6. I was playing at Excalibur in Las Vegas one night when the dealer was on a roll. A lady to my right complained, "Those are bust cards. So bust!"

The problem is that we see a 6 face up and we automatically start thinking "16" instead of 6. Now, a 16 is an entirely different matter. An Ace, 2, 3, 4 or 5 gives the dealer 17 or better, but the other eight denominations—6, 7, 8, 9, 10, Jack, Queen or King—bust the hand. With 16, the dealer busts 62 percent of the time. But less than a third of the cards in the deck—30.8 percent of them, to be precise—have values of 10. Most of the time that he has a 6 showing, the dealer will be drawing to a two-card total that is more advantageous than 16.

2. False. The "sure thing" of insuring a blackjack is a myth perpetuated by dealers from New Jersey to Indiana to Missouri to Nevada, one that costs players thousands of dollars every day.

In answer number 1 in this section, I mentioned that 30.8 percent of the cards have values of 10. In order for insurance to be a break-even proposition, a full one-third of the cards would have to be 10s.

Let's say you play 1,000 hands, with a $10 bet on each one. Each time, you're dealt a blackjack and the dealer has an Ace face up. "You should insure that hand," the dealer tells you. "It's the only sure winner in the casino."

You'll remember from *Blackjack Hand Number 2: Definitions*, that insurance is a bet that the dealer has blackjack, and to insure a blackjack you need only call out, "even money." You give up a chance at a 3-2 payoff on blackjack, but you guarantee that you win $10 on every hand, even if the dealer also has blackjack. By insuring, you win $10 on each of the 1,000 hands, for $10,000 in winnings. But let's say you decline insurance. You'll take your chances, accept that you'll win nothing when the dealer has blackjack, but win $15 instead of only $10 whenever the dealer does not have a 10-value card face down. In the long run, per 1,000 hands that start with an Ace, the dealer will have a 10-value card face down 308 times. That leaves 692 winning hands, each one winning $15. And that comes to $10,380 in profits. On the average, $10 bet for each of 1,000 hands that start with an Ace, the player costs himself $380 by taking the "sure thing" insurance bet.

3. True. Blackjack can be beaten, but not easily. Players who count cards can gain a small edge over the house, but it takes knowledge, discipline, bankroll, and practice, practice, practice.

Without any one of those factors, a card counter's edge disappears. First off, the player must know how to count cards and apply that knowledge to his betting and playing strategies. He must have the discipline to stick to it, not get sloppy in his technique or lose concentration. He must have a large enough bankroll to make playing a card-counting system feasible: if you're at a table with $5 minimum bets and the count tells you that the situation is favorable for a 10-unit bet, you'd better be prepared to bet $50 or you're giving away your edge. A player who sits down at a $5 table with $100 will not be able to make the size bets necessary to get an edge on the casino.

How big an edge can a card counter get? Perhaps 1 percent, maybe a fraction more, depending on house rules, what percentage of the cards are dealt out between shuffles and how large a spread from his minimum to his maximum bet the casino will allow. That's not a lot. One colleague told me that he tried scraping out a living counting cards in low minimum games. He found he was playing long hours every day, running himself into the ground until he finally figured that on an hourly basis he was making less money than he could at a fast-food restaurant. It's a hard way to make an easy living.

Yes, it's possible to get an edge on the house, but unless you have a very large bankroll already, the biggest rewards from counting cards come from the personal satisfaction of being able to beat the casino at its own game.

4. True. The player is just as likely as the dealer to get blackjack. It happens an average of about once per 21 hands.

Sometimes even the casino doesn't realize just how often blackjack comes up, or how important it is to the overall odds of the game. In *Blackjack Hand Number 4: Good Rules, Bad Rules*, we'll look at the effect of having blackjack pay 2-1, and at the effect of it paying only even money instead of the normal 3-2.

For a time, the Continental in Las Vegas so misunderstood how often blackjack occurs that it just about gave away the store. It ran a special promotion: Hit two blackjacks in a row and win a $500 bonus. The only requirement was that the player bet at least $5 per hand.

To figure how often a player should hit two consecutive blackjacks, multiply that once-per-21 hands frequency by itself. You get two blackjacks in a row about once per 441 hands—not an exact figure, but close enough. At $5 per hand for 441 hands, the average player could expect to lose about $50, and a basic strategy player could expect to lose about $10. At that rate, a $500 bonus seems like a pretty good incentive to take the day off work and play cards instead. It didn't take long for the Continental to reduce its bonus, then reduce it again before finally eliminating it.

5. False. Assuming that unseen dealer cards are 10s will draw the player into a few strategy mistakes. For example, if the player has 12 and the dealer shows a 3, many players—a majority of those I've observed—will stand. They figure the dealer most likely has 13, and another 10 will bust him. But that precise combination—a 10 down, then hitting with another 10—will occur only a little more than 9 percent of the time. Showing a 3, the dealer will bust about 38 percent of the time. Given that we can only bust our 12 by drawing a 10-value card, which account for 30.8 percent of the cards, our best play against a 3 is to hit on 12.

That being said, assuming 10 down will give us a fairly accurate guideline for many hands. If the dealer's face-up card is a 7 or higher, we do work on the assumption he'll wind up with 17 or better. His two-card total won't always be there, but he'll get there nearly three-quarters of the time with a 7, and more than that with an 8, 9, 10-value or Ace. The dealer makes his hand such an overwhelming percentage of the time with those cards that we must hit 12 through 16, even though we risk busting in one card.

On the flip side, when the dealer shows 4, 5 or 6, his percentage of busts is high enough that it makes it imprudent to risk busting our own 12s or higher. The same is true when the dealer shows 2 or 3 and we have 13 or higher—we balance the risks of busting, and decide ours is too high. We stand against 2 or 3 with 13 or higher, but hit with 12.

6. False. It just seems like we draw 10s every time we hit a 12. There's a little selective memory at work here. One day I was playing at the Flamingo Hilton in Las Vegas, and had one of those streaks. Within about 15 hands, I had four 12s busted when I drew 10-value cards. I could only shake my head, and the dealer sympathized. "That's the way it always works for me when I'm on the other side of the table," she commiserated. "I only bust when I'm playing."

Now, there's no reason for the player to bust those 12s any

more often than the dealer does. Hit a 12, and you should draw a 10, Jack, Queen or King to bust an average of 30.8 percent of the time, even though it seems like it happens a lot more.

I decided to keep track. I took a memo pad from my hotel room in Las Vegas and carried it in my pocket. I kept mental track of how many times I hit 12, and how many times I busted, and each time I left the table, I jotted it down. Fifty-three more times on that trip I hit 12, and on 13 times, the next card was a 10 that busted me. For that short period, I busted less than a quarter of the time I hit 12.

That's not a long enough sample to prove anything, but it put my mind at rest. Without that little exercise, I probably would have left remembering the earlier streak, and maybe I'd have been like so many others who are a little gun-shy about hitting 12 in the proper situations. But the mathematics of the game say that in the long run, I should bust that hand an average of 30.8 percent of the time. The math is right.

7. False. How many times have you heard another player muse that 2s are lousy for the player, but great for the dealer? It is true that in general, a high concentration of high cards in the cards remaining to be dealt favors the player and a high concentration of low cards favors the dealer. That is the main underpinning of card counting—counters raise their bets when blackjacks are most likely and lower them when blackjacks are least likely.

But in the specific situation of starting with a 2 vs. starting with an Ace, the dealer is more likely to wind up with a good hand when he starts with an Ace. When starting with a 2, he'll bust about 35 percent of the time, but bust only about 11 percent of the time when starting with an Ace.

The dealer who starts with a 2 is no more likely to pull a good hand than a player who starts with a 2. Of course, within a few seconds of starting with a 2, the player sees his second card, so he rarely thinks of his hand as starting with a 2.

8. True. Given a normal set of rules, the players should always split Aces or 8s. Sometimes it's because splitting the pair gives the player an edge—splitting Aces when the dealer shows a

5 is a very profitable situation, for example. Sometimes we split as a defensive measure: we split 8s when the dealer shows a 10 because 16 is such a lousy hand to play. When we split 8s against a 10, we're still an underdog on each hand. Sometimes we'll draw a 10 on each 8, have two 18s and lose them both when the dealer turns a 10 up for a 20. But overall, we'll lose less money by splitting the 8s than we will by playing one hand out as a 16 instead.

9. False. If I found a dealer I thought was skillful enough to manipulate where the good cards were going, I'd leave that casino. I'd certainly have to suspect that skill would be used against me a lot more often that it would benefit me. Either way, using such a skill in the casino is illegal, and if caught the dealer would lose his license and be prosecuted.

In most casinos, tips are pooled. All the dealers on a given shift split the shift's tips equally. That evens things out so that someone who's been kept on her toes all day at the $2 tables doesn't walk away with nothing while another dealer fortunate enough to have a generous high roller at her table all day makes a big score.

The most common way to tip a blackjack dealer is to place a bet for the dealer at the front of the player's betting spot. Some card counters seek out the relatively few casinos that allow dealers to keep their own tips. It's not because they think the dealer will direct cards their way. They hope to play a little cat and mouse game to lure the dealer into dealing deeper into the deck. This works only if the casino has a hand-held single-deck or double-deck game in which the dealer has some discretion as to when to shuffle. The player might put out a tip to the dealer as a signal that the count is good, that he wants another hand dealt before the shuffle. If the dealer doesn't take the bait and shuffles instead, the player withdraws the tip. Then the player awaits the next favorable situation at about time to shuffle, and tries again. Sometimes the dealer plays along; sometimes she doesn't.

10. False. Card counting has never been held to be illegal by any court in the United States. It is merely skillful play. However, the casinos don't have to just sit back and allow players to get an edge on their games. They may take counter measures, depending on their state laws and gaming regulations. In Nevada, courts have long held that casinos are private clubs and may refuse service to any customer for any reason. Nevada casinos can bar card counters from playing. Some are more aggressive about barring than others—the Barbary Coast on the Strip has the reputation of being the quickest heave-ho in town.

Others have a more of a laissez-faire policy—35 years of dealing with counters has taught them that most either aren't good enough or don't have a large enough bankroll to do the casino any real damage. And the idea that the casino offers a game that can be beaten is good for business. If card counting and the idea that blackjack can be beaten were ever stamped out, the game probably would suffer a serious decline. But even the most hands-off casinos have to be on the alert for the few counters who can hurt them, and for big-bankrolled card-counting teams.

Often, casinos will try other measures without resorting to barring players. Some might shuffle the cards early. Others might limit a player's bet size. Counters live off making big bets when the cards remaining to be dealt favor the player. Limit the bet size, and the counter can't make any money.

The casino counter measure with which I have the biggest problem is the early shuffle. That's because it doesn't just hinder the counter, it changes the odds against all players at the table. If a casino supervisor counts along and instructs the dealer to shuffle whenever the count is favorable—as occasionally happens—then all players at the table are playing only in situations that favor the house. They don't get the good times that normally come with the bad times by random chance. I have little problem with limiting the ability of the card counter to hurt the house, but selective shuffling by the house so that all players face negative situations all the time is cheating.

Blackjack Hand Number 4: Good Rules, Bad Rules

With one or two exceptions, it won't be too difficult here to pick out which rules benefit the players and which ones are designed to give the house a bigger edge. But as you decide "good" or "bad" for the player, think about why each rule is a help or hindrance, and just how big an effect each one has on the game.

In my answers, I'm going to tell you by how many percent (or tenths or hundredths of a percent) each rule raises or lowers the house edge. Don't get too hung up on the numbers, and don't let them overwhelm you. Understanding which rules help the player and which ones hinder can be important in choosing a game. The numbers are simply a guide to which rules have the bigger effect.

1. Dealer hits soft 17
2. Player may resplit Aces
3. Player may double down after splitting pairs
4. Dealer wins ties
5. Double down on 9, 10 and 11 only
6. Blackjack pays 2-1
7. Player may double down on three-card totals
8. No resplitting of pairs
9. Late surrender
10. Early surrender
11. Insurance
12. One deck

13. Two decks
14. Six decks
15. Dealer blackjack wins split-pair and double down bets
16. Six cards totaling 21 or under win
17. Five-card Charlie (five cards totaling 21 pay 2-1)
18. 6-7-8 pays 2-1
19. 7-7-7 pays 2-1
20. All player 21s push when the dealer has an Ace face down to complete a blackjack
21. Blackjacks pay even money

Blackjack Hand Number 4: Good Hand, Bad Hand Answers

1. Bad. Whether the dealer hits or stands on soft 17 is one of the most important variable rules in blackjack. All by itself, having the dealer hit soft 17 adds two-tenths of a percent to the house advantage, which means that on the average, the casino wins an extra 20 cents for every $100 played.

As with most of the rules discussed in this section, the effect on the house edge is an average. There are slight variations depending on the number of decks in play. In *The Theory of Blackjack*, Peter Griffin points out that the dealer hitting soft 17 increases the house edge by 0.19 percent in a single-deck game, but increases it by 0.22 percent with infinite decks. We'll stick with 0.2 for the most part. Now, a 0.2 percent increase in the house edge might not sound like much, but we're dealing with a game in which the entire house advantage against a player who knows his stuff is measured in tenths of a percent. In a common six-deck game, the whole house edge against a player who uses basic strategy hovers around 0.5 percent, depending on house rules.

Or take a single-deck game in which the dealer stands on all 17s and the player may double down on any first two cards. Against a basic strategy player, there is no house edge in this game. In fact, there's a miniscule player edge of 0.01 percent. Just by having the dealer hit soft 17, the house takes an edge of 0.2 percent. (To be more precise, 0.18 percent. But let's stay with round numbers as much as possible.) A $10 bettor, playing 50 hands per hour at a crowded table, goes from breaking even in an average hour when the dealer stands on all 17s to losing $1 per hour if the dealer hits soft 17.

The effect gets larger at higher limits because with fewer players at tables with high minimum bets, hands are completed faster and more hands are dealt per hour. A $100-a-hand bettor, playing 200 hands per hour, goes from a break-even situation if the dealer stands on all 17s to losses of $40 per hour if the dealer hits soft 17.

Sometimes players don't recognize this as a bad rule at all, much less realize it's one of the toughest blackjack variations the casino can deal at you. I had this discussion with a friend of the family recently. He insisted that the most frustrating loss in black-jack comes when the dealer has a 6 face up, the player stands on 16, and the dealer then turns up an Ace for 17. At least, he claimed, if the house rules call for the dealer to hit soft 17, there's still a chance the dealer could bust. And it's true that the dealer does bust more often if he hits soft 17. The flip side, though, is that much more common than winning with a surprise Ace under a 6, hitting soft 17 will enable the dealer to make totals of 18 through 21 to beat you in hands you'd otherwise win. The bottom line is that 17 is not a very good hand, and giving the dealer a chance to improve it benefits only the house.

2. Good. On my list of the most frustrating casino hands, there'd be a place reserved for receiving an Ace on another split Ace. You've split your pair and are hoping for a high card, and bam! There it is. The highest card in the deck. But if the casino doesn't allow you to resplit Aces—and many don't—all it does for you in this situation is stick you with a 12 that can't win unless the dealer busts. The gain from being allowed to resplit Aces isn't enormous—only 0.07 percent—but I find the gain in peace of mind to be much larger.

3. Good. Allowing the player to double down after splitting pairs is important enough that it makes a difference in basic strategy for pair splits. For example, in a multiple-deck game, if you're dealt a pair of 4s and the dealer's face-up card is a 6, you split the pair if you are allowed to double after splits. If house rules don't allow doubling after splits, you just hit the 8 instead. The net gain for being allowed to double after splits is 0.1 percent. It's a pretty common option in multiple-deck games, but rare where a single deck is used.

4. Really, really bad. Sometimes at charity casino nights you'll find a game in which the house wins all ties. This is an enormous advantage to the house, so big that you'll not want to play in such games unless they're to benefit an organization for which you'd be willing to write a check anyway. This no-push rule all by itself gives the house an advantage of 8.8 percent. If all other rules were balanced equally between the player and dealer, in the long run the house would keep an average of $8.80 of every $100 you wagered. This rule alone would make blackjack one of the worst bets in the casino.

You'll see the house-wins-ties rule in effect in a regular casino only if there are powerful compensating rules in the players' favor. The house wins ties in a game called Double Exposure Blackjack that was introduced at Vegas World in Las Vegas. (Vegas World since has been torn down to make way for Stratosphere Tower, which continues to offer Double Exposure.) But in Double Exposure, all dealer cards are dealt face-up, mitigating the effect of no-push.

5. Bad—at least for most players. I've seen players double down on hard 12, risking busting with one hit. I've seen players double on 8 when the dealer showed a 7, gambling that they'd win 18-17 if they'd hit a 10 AND the dealer had a 10 face down. (The chance of it happening so neatly is between 9.5 and 10.7 percent, depending on the number of decks in play.) At the Tropicana in Las Vegas many years ago, I even saw someone double down on a blackjack, tossing away their 3-2 payoffs.

Players like these actually benefit from a rule restricting double downs to 9, 10 and 11. But for those who double down wisely, this restriction costs 0.1 percent. A few even more restrictive casinos limit doubling to two-card totals of 10 or 11. That costs the player 0.2 percent, making this just as bad a rule as having the dealer hit soft 17.

When we discuss doubling hands other than 9, 10 or 11, we're really talking about soft hands. We want to be able to double Ace-4, for example, when the dealer shows a 4, 5, or 6. In single-deck games, the player will want to double on hard 8 against a 5 or 6, but the more important loss when doubling is restricted to 9, 10 or 11 is the ability to double down on soft hands.

6. Great, and extremely rare. When this rule pops up, it usually doesn't take long for it to disappear.

That's just what happened at the Alton Belle on the Illinois side of the Mississippi River a few years ago. Word got out fast on the blackjack players' grapevine that the casino was paying 2-1 instead of 3-2 on blackjack, and Alton Belle found itself swamped with big money players. Casino managers quickly found this was no blessing. The big players were cleaning out the chip trays. Soon, Alton Belle reverted to 3-2 payoffs on blackjack.

It's no wonder. Paying 2-1 on blackjacks is a 2.3 percent gain for the player. Think about that: a 2.3 percent player gain in a game that starts with only a 0.5 percent house advantage. That leaves a player edge of 1.8 percent, which is more than triple the house edge minus this rule. A $10-a-hand player, playing 50 hands an hour, goes from an expected loss of $2.50 per hour to an expected win of $9 per hour.

Alton Belle went back to the well with this one a little more than a year after its initial disaster. This time the casino covered itself a little better. The 2-1 blackjack payoffs were part of a Two-for-Tuesday promotion that included double odds on craps and double points for slot club members. On top of that, the 2-1 payoffs were limited to the first $25 of a player's bet, meaning that a player who hit blackjack with $100 on the table was paid 2-1 on the first $25 and 3-2 on the remaining $75. That prevented wholesale carnage and left a nice little promotion that rewarded loyal local players without attracting big money from all over the country.

7. Good. You have a 2 and a 3, and you're dealt a 6 for a three-card 11. Wouldn't you like the chance to double down now? Most of the time you'll have to settle for a hit, but not at the Las Vegas Club in downtown Las Vegas. There you can double down. It's an option worth 0.2 percent to the player. That offsets the casino's 0.2 percent edge if it hits soft 17, which the Las Vegas Club does.

8. Bad. You're dealt a pair of 8s, and you split. It doesn't matter what the dealer's up card is, the optimal play is to split 8s. Now you're dealt another 8. What's the best play? Split them again. You don't want to be stuck playing two 8s as a 16. But some casinos won't allow you to resplit pairs. Ugh! It's a 0.1 percent increase in the house advantage.

9. Good. You're dealt a 9 and a 7, and the dealer shows an Ace. Bad news. If you hit, there's better than a 60 percent chance that you bust, and even if you make 17 or better, you could lose to the dealer's better total. In fact, you'll lose more than 80 percent of the time. If you stand, there's about an 88 percent chance that the dealer will make 17 or better and beat you.

When you're under the gun like that, it's actually to your advantage to surrender (give up half your bet instead of playing out the hand). With late surrender, you have to wait until the dealer checks to see if he has blackjack before you surrender. If he has blackjack, you lose your whole bet.

There are only a few situations when it's to your advantage to surrender. Surrender hard 15 if the dealer has a 10, and hard 16 when the dealer has a 9, 10 or 16. Exception: do not surrender a pair of 8s. Split instead. Surrendering under those conditions is a modest 0.06 percent gain for the player.

10. Really good, and so rare it's almost nonexistent. When you can surrender before the dealer checks for blackjack, it's a 0.6 percent gain for the player. That'll wipe out a lot of 0.2 percent or 0.1 percent negative rules.

The Holiday Inn Boardwalk on the Las Vegas Strip offered early surrender for a short time in 1997. It turned a mediocre six-deck game into a good one, with a small player edge of less than 0.1 percent. It also turned Boardwalk's two-decker into a terrific

game for ordinary players, and it left casino supervisors so para-
noid about attracting card counters that the atmosphere was too
tense for all but the most oblivious. Early surrender disappeared
from the Boardwalk within a few months.

11. Good, in the sense that any option is good if the player
knows how to use it, but bad in that it's an option that should
never be used unless the player is counting cards.

Insurance is a bet that the dealer has blackjack. If the dealer
has an Ace face up, the player may make an insurance bet half
the size of his bet on his own hand. If the dealer then has blackjack, the insurance bet is paid at 2-1. That would be an even
proposition if one-third of the cards in the deck had values of 10.
Then the dealer would have blackjack an average of once for
every three times he started with an Ace face up. For every three
insurance bets, the player would lose two when the dealer did
not have blackjack, but win two units for the 2-1 payback when
he did. Everybody would be all even. But only 30.8 percent of
the cards in the deck have values of 10, and that makes insurance
a losing proposition for the player. The only players who should
take insurance are card counters who know that an excess of
small cards have been played and that a third or more of the remaining cards have values of 10.

This advice also applies in situations where a player is using
insurance to take even money on blackjacks, as described in our
definitions section (*Blackjack Hand Number 2: Definitions*).
Nearly every dealer I've encountered, from Indiana to Mississippi
to Missouri to Nevada advises players to insure blackjacks. "It's
the only sure bet in the casino," they'll tell you. And nearly every
dealer I've encountered is wrong. You're costing yourself money
in the long run if you give up your 3-2 payoff on blackjack for the
sake of a "sure thing" that occurs only 30.8 percent of the time
instead of the 33 percent needed to break even.

12. Good. One deck is where blackjack started, and I love a
good single-deck game. But you're probably getting the idea by
now that there's more to putting together a good or bad game
than just the number of decks in play.

13. Good, or bad. It depends on where you're playing. If you're surrounded by a lot of single-deck blackjack, then double-deck with equal rules is tougher. If you're in an area with only six-deck or eight-deck games, then a two-decker is a breath of fresh air. See below.

14. Bad. When the card counting revolution stirred up in the 1960s, one of the first casino responses was to increase the number of decks in play. Each deck added makes the game a little tougher. In fact, among common rules, the number of decks in play has the biggest impact on the game.

The biggest increase in the house edge comes in going from one deck to two. That increases the house edge by 0.38 percent, or just about double the increase from having the dealer hit soft 17. Increases in the house edge slow considerably after that: compared with a single-deck game, using six decks adds just 0.5 percent to the house edge.

I frequently receive letters from readers asking whether increasing the number of decks increases the house edge against everyone, or just against card counters. The increase impacts everyone, I assure them, for a couple of reasons that don't seem to make sense at a glance. First, there are more blackjacks in single-deck games than in multiple-deckers. "How could that be," one man asked at a seminar I gave. "The percentages of 10s and Aces are the same no matter how many decks there are."

The answer is that the effect of removing each card from play affects the percentages of remaining cards to a greater extent in a single-deck game than when multiple decks are used. Let's say the player receives an Ace as his first card. In a single-deck game, that's one card out of fifty-two. There are sixteen cards with values of 10 among the fifty-one other cards. That's 31.4 percent of the remaining cards that complete a blackjack. Now assume an eight-deck game, again with the player starting with an Ace. That's one card out of 416. There are 128 10-value cards among the remaining 415. That's only 30.8 percent that will complete a blackjack. "But that applies equally to the player and the dealer," the fellow at my seminar protested. "OK, there will

be more blackjacks, but there will be more for the dealer, too."
True enough. But player blackjacks pay 3-2. You don't pay the
dealer any bonus when he gets one. Anything that increases
blackjacks is good for the player.

The second reason is similar. In double-down situations,
you'll get the card you need more frequently in single-deck
games. Let's say you start with a two-card 11—it doesn't matter if
it consists of 6-5, 7-4, 8-3 or 9-2. In a single-deck game, there are
fifty remaining cards, and sixteen of them, or 32 percent, are 10-
values that will give you 21 on your double down. In an eight-
deck game, start with a two-card 11 and there are 414 remaining
cards, and 128 of them, or 30.9 percent, are the desired 10s,
Jacks, Queens and Kings.

All other rules being equal, the fewer the decks, the better
for the player. Of course, when the casino starts to mix and match
rules, it gets more complicated.

15. Bad, and fortunately rare in American casinos. A dealer
blackjack taking both split bets or both double down bets happens most frequently overseas or on cruise ships. Usually it happens in a game in which the dealer does not start with a hole
card. On the initial deal, the dealer takes only a face up card. He
doesn't take a second card until all players have completed their
hands.

In that situation, players will split pairs or make double
down bets without knowing whether the dealer has blackjack. In
most American casinos, the dealer checks whenever he has an
Ace or 10 up, and stops the hand if he has blackjack. The splits
and doubles never get made. Even in those casinos that don't
check under 10 (I've never seen one in this country that doesn't
check under Aces), split and double bets are almost always returned to the player if the dealer has blackjack. But in overseas
no-hole card games, the splits and doubles are made before the
dealer gets a second card. If that second card completes a blackjack, the house takes all bets on the table, including splits and
doubles. This adds 0.1 percent to the house edge.

16. Good. There's no waiting for the dealer to play out his hand. If you have six cards totaling 21 or under, you win. (Of course, if the dealer has blackjack, play will stopped after the initial deal and you'll lose before you get this far.) It's about a 0.1 percent gain for the player. The rule isn't common, but at any given time it's offered at a few Nevada casinos—notably the Las Vegas Club. It's also featured on the video blackjack games on the new Multi-Pay Plus multiple-game machines manufactured by Williams.

17. Good. Five-card Charlies that pay 2-1 on five-card 21s are worth 0.2 percent to the player. This is not a common rule, although first-time casino visitors seem surprised when they find it's not available. I once sat next to a fellow at Slots o' Fun next to Circus Circus in Las Vegas who was beyond disbelief when he received no bonus on his five-card 21. Seems the guys in his home poker game sometimes dealt blackjack and always paid five-card Charlies. Of course, the same fellow was beyond belief a little later when the dealer picked up his bet when he had a four-card 21 vs. the dealer's blackjack. It took the whole table to explain that a two-card 21 beat anything except another two-card 21.

18 and 19. Good. Bonuses like 2-1 on 6-7-8 or 7-7-7 seem to crop up more frequently in Northern Nevada than anywhere else. Look for them if you're in Reno and Lake Tahoe, and sometimes in Elko or Wendover, Nevada. The better bonus of the two is 2-1 on 6-7-8. That gains the player 0.2 percent. It's not as common to hit 7-7-7, and the bonus is worth only 0.02 percent to the player—a tenth the value of 6-7-8.

19. See 18.

20. Good. This one caught me by surprise on a trip to Tunica County, Mississippi. I'd heard that Mississippi gambling was really competitive, but until I actually saw it I didn't realize just what that meant to the player. I checked out Hollywood, Harrah's, Sam's Town, Fitzgerald's, the Horseshoe and was astounded. Craps with 20x odds at a time that the most liberal Las Vegas casinos were offering 10x odds. Single-zero roulette.

Then there was blackjack. I sat down at a single-deck table

at Harrah's. The dealer hit soft 17, but then there was this funky rule that if the dealer showed a 10 and I had a 21 with any number of cards, I couldn't lose. If my 21 beat the dealer, great, I won. But if the dealer turned over an Ace for a two-card 21, I didn't lose, I pushed. It's a gain of 0.17 percent for the player, and it cut the house edge on that Harrah's single-deck game all the way to a negligible 0.01 percent against a basic strategy player.

21. Awful. Remember from answer number 6 how the player gains 2.3 percent if the house pays 2-1 instead of 3-2 on blackjack? Remember how good that makes the game for the player. Having blackjack pay even money is that rule's evil twin. This one COSTS the player 2.3 percent.

Outside of charity games and Double Exposure blackjack, it's rare to see blackjacks pay only even money. But it crops up occasionally at regular blackjack games. When it does, the player should move swiftly in the opposite direction. In 1996, in the waning days before the closing of the Bourbon Street off the Las Vegas Strip, that casino had a single-deck table in which the dealer hit soft 17 and blackjacks paid only even money. That's a hefty house edge of 2.5 percent against a basic strategy player. Anyone who really knew the game wouldn't have played it.

Blackjack Hand Number 5: Good Game, Bad Game

Modern blackjack is a mix-and-match game, with each casino balancing good rules and bad from a list including those we discussed in the last section.

Below, 10 sets of rules are listed, drawn from real games available in casinos in the late 1990s. Three of them are good games, with a house edge of less than 0.2 percent against a basic strategy player. Four of them are moderate, with house edges from 0.4 percent down to 0.25 percent. And three are tough games, with house edges of 0.53 percent or more.

See if you can divide these games into three groups: good, moderate and tough games to play.

A. Six decks, dealer stands on all 17s, player may double after splits, player may resplit Aces, late surrender offered.

B. One deck, dealer stands on all 17s, blackjacks pay even money.

C. Two decks, dealer hits soft 17, player may double after splits.

D. Two decks, dealer hits soft 17, double down on 9, 10 or 11 only, no resplits.

E. One deck, dealer stands on all 17s, double down on 9, 10 or 11 only.

F. Six decks, dealer hits soft 17, player may double down on any first two or three cards, six cards of 21 or under is an automatic winner, player may double after splits, player may resplit Aces, late surrender offered.

G. One deck, dealer hits soft 17.

H. Six decks, dealer hits soft 17, player may double after splits.

I. Six decks, all cards dealt face up, all player blackjacks win, even against dealer blackjacks, but blackjacks pay even money, house wins ties, no resplits, Ace-Jack of hearts pays 2-1, 6-7-8 pays 2-1.

J. Eight decks, dealer stands on all 17s, no resplits, player may double after splits, late surrender offered.

Blackjack Hand Number 5: Good Game, Bad Game Answers

Good games: E, F and G.
Moderate games: A, C, I and J.
Tough games: B, D and H.

All the rules we discussed in *Blackjack Hand Number 4: Good Rules, Bad Rules* work together to determine how big an edge the house has against a basic strategy player. To show how this works, let's take a look at game A. Starting from zero, we add 0.5 percent to the house edge because six decks are in use. But we gain 0.1 percent because we can double after splits, 0.7 percent because we can resplit Aces and 0.7 percent for late surrender. That all adds up to a house edge of 0.26 percent.

Purists will note that figure is very close, but not precise (the precise figure is 0.25 percent). The effects of rounding and the fact that some rules have a slightly different impact depending on the number of decks in play can affect the bottom line by a few hundredths of a percent.

All but the most negative rules can be offset by adding a few positives. The three good games were chosen as extremes—single deck games and six-deckers—games using one, two and six decks—so that we'd have games in which the dealer stands on all 17s and games in which the dealer hits soft 17. A six-deck game in which the dealer hits soft 17 is a rugged way to start. A general rule of thumb is that you should avoid multiple-deck games in which the dealer hits soft 17. Yet in game F we have a game with both those negative rules that ranks with the good games. Why?

Game F is a special case. That's the game at the Las Vegas Club, which boasts "The World's Most Liberal Blackjack Rules." Layering on all those player options yields a game with a house edge of just 0.12 percent against a basic strategy player. A $10 bettor playing 50 hands per hour has expected average losses of just 60 cents per hour, if he knows how to use all the rules wisely.

Game E is an odd little mix from Baldini's in Sparks, Nevada. Most casinos that deal single-deck claim an edge by having the dealer hit soft 17. (Single-deck blackjack in which the dealer stands on all 17s and there are no negative side rules is just about an even game, with a 0.01 percent player edge.) But the Baldini's game gives the house an edge by limiting double downs to 9, 10 or 11 instead. That gives the casino a 0.13 percent advantage.

Game G is the most common single-deck game around. Many casinos in downtown Las Vegas offer this one, and it's also common in northern Nevada. Hitting soft 17 with no other exotic rules brings the house edge to 0.18 percent.

Moving to the moderate games, game A (0.25 percent house edge) has popped up in several casinos in Nevada, and game C (0.39 percent) is fairly common in Nevada and Mississippi.

The eight-deck game J (0.4 percent) is an example of what's available in Atlantic City. It's rare that an Atlantic City casino offers a game with fewer than six decks, and eight decks are more common than six. It's standard for the dealer to stand on all 17s, but nearly every casino in Atlantic City either bars resplits or limits the player to one resplit for a total of three hands. In checking out casinos in newer gaming jurisdictions, I've found that you can tell where the management team is from by checking out the blackjack rules. At its simplest, if the casino bars resplits or limits the player to one resplit, management was trained in New Jersey; if the player is allowed to resplit twice or more, management was trained in Nevada. That doesn't always hold true, but check it out sometime if you're visiting a riverboat or a Native American operation.

The rare one in this group is game I. That's the best version of Double Exposure Blackjack I've ever seen, dealt at the Lady Luck in downtown Las Vegas. Some Double Exposure games put restrictions on double downs. Being able to double on any first two cards is an important weapon in Double Exposure. With all dealer cards dealt face up, you'll know if the dealer has 16 in his first two cards. When he does, you'll want your money on the table. Double down on hard 5, if the casino will let you. The Lady Luck allows that play, and has a house edge on Double Exposure of just 0.35 percent. Other Double Exposure games sometimes quadruple that edge.

In almost any gaming jurisdiction, you'll find a casino that hits soft 17 in a six-deck game without layering on positive rules to make up for it. Unless you're stuck in one casino, there's no reason to play game H, with a 0.62 percent house edge. If you're in Nevada or Mississippi, walk next door and find a game with better rules. If you're on a riverboat or in a Native American casino miles from another place to play, keep it in mind the next time you choose a casino.

Game D (0.68 percent) is a tough set of double-deck rules I encountered at the Hollywood Casino in Aurora, Illinois. When the casino goes to multiple decks, there is little reason to also hit soft 17. To then limit double downs to two-card totals of 9, 10 or 11 and bar resplits of pairs is just piling on. The odd thing is that the same casino offers a moderate six-deck game in which the dealer stands on all 17s and the player may double after splits. House edge: 0.4 percent. For those who think fewer decks means a better game, here's proof within one casino that it's not always so.

Game B, of course, is the toughest of the tough. A single-deck game in which the dealer stands on all 17s is terrific. I see those two rules and figure I can play all day. Then comes the hammer: blackjacks pay even money. This one at the Lady Luck in Biloxi, Mississippi, had a house edge of 2.31 percent, nearly 20 times the edge on the Las Vegas Club's six-deck game detailed at the beginning of this hand.

Blackjack Hand Number 6: Strategies for Hard Totals

The following twenty-one situations will give you a chance to test your knowledge of blackjack basic strategy for hard totals. Assume a multiple-deck game in which the player may double down on any first two cards. Pick the best option for each player total against the dealer's given face-up card.

1. **Player has 12. Dealer shows a 2.**

    A. Hit
    B. Stand
    C. Double down

2. **Player has 12. Dealer shows a 6**

    A. Hit
    B. Stand
    C. Double down

3. **Player has 12. Dealer shows a 9.**

    A. Hit
    B. Stand
    C. Double down

4. **Player has 13. Dealer shows a 2.**

    A. Hit
    B. Stand
    C. Double down

5. Player has 11. Dealer shows an Ace

    A. Hit
    B. Stand
    C. Double down

6. Player has 11. Dealer shows a 10.

    A. Hit
    B. Stand
    C. Double down

7. Player has 16. Dealer shows a 6.

    A. Hit
    B. Stand
    C. Double down

8. Player has 16. Dealer shows a 7.

    A. Hit
    B. Stand
    C. Double down

9. Player has 16. Dealer shows a 10.

    A. Hit
    B. Stand
    C. Double down

10. Player has 10. Dealer shows a 9.

    A. Hit
    B. Stand
    C. Double down

11. Player has 10. Dealer shows a 10.

    A. Hit
    B. Stand
    C. Double down

12. Player has 10. Dealer shows an Ace.

    A. Hit

B. Stand

C. Double down

13. Player has 14. Dealer shows a 7.

A. Hit

B. Stand

C. Double down

14. Player has 15. Dealer shows an 8.

A. Hit

B. Stand

C. Double down

15. Player has 9. Dealer shows a 2.

A. Hit

B. Stand

C. Double down

16. Player has 9. Dealer shows a 6.

A. Hit

B. Stand

C. Double down

17. Player has 9. Dealer shows a 7.

A. Hit

B. Stand

C. Double down

18. Player has 8. Dealer shows a 6.

A. Hit

B. Stand

C. Double down

19. Player has 8. Dealer shows a 7.

A. Hit

B. Stand

C. Double down

20. Player has 17. Dealer shows an Ace.

    A. Hit

    B. Stand

    C. Take insurance

21. Player has 20. Dealer shows an Ace.

    A. Hit

    B. Stand

    C. Take insurance

Blackjack Hand Number 6: Strategies for Hard Totals Answers

1. A. (See answer number 3)

2. B. (See answer number 3)

3. A. Hard 12 is a borderline hand. We'll bust often enough that we don't want to risk it if the dealer's chance of busting is large enough. But we must hit if the dealer is so likely to make a hand of 17 or better that we have little chance of winning if we stand. If the dealer shows a 2 or a 3, we hit hard 12. Other players, and even the dealer, may grumble when you do it, but you'll save yourself some money. This is not a profit opportunity; it's a chance to cut your losses. By hitting hard 12 against 2, you'll cut your average losses to a little more than $250 per $1,000 wagered in this situation; if you stand instead, you'll lose a little less than $290 per $1,000 wagered.

When the dealer shows a 4, 5 or 6, the chance of the dealer busting grows large enough that we're better off standing on the 12 than risking busting ourselves. Then, when the dealer's up card is 7 or higher, the probability that he'll make 17 or better grows so large that we have to hit to give ourselves a fighting chance.

The large segment of players who ALMOST know basic strategy will stand on 12 against 2 through 6 and hit if the dealer has 7 through Ace. That's not a terrible strategy. In fact, I have often recommended to beginners that they learn a quick version of basic that makes them better than most players and gets the house edge on a multiple-deck game down to less than 1 percent. They just miss a few fine points, including hitting 12 when the dealer shows a 2 or 3.

The quick version of basic strategy is as follows:

- Always stand on 17 through 21, except hit soft 17.
- Hit 12 through 16 when the dealer shows a 7 or better.
- Stand on 12 through 16 when the dealer shows a 2, 3, 4, 5 or 6.
- Always split Aces and 8s.
- Double down on 10 or 11 unless the dealer shows a 10 or Ace.
- Hit any total of 9 or less.

That's not perfect. It misses several fine points. You'll pick up some of the fine points in these answers, like hitting 12 when the dealer shows a 2 or 3.

4. B. A similar quiz in my newspaper column once drew a flood of letters. "I don't understand," one said. "Why do you hit 12 against a 3 but not 13 against a 2. Isn't that the same thing?'"It is not the same. We'll bust 13 in one hit a lot more often than we'll bust 12—38.5 percent of the time vs. 30.8 percent. That heightened risk of busting means that starting with 13 and running through 16, we stand whenever the dealer shows 2 through 12 and hit only when he shows 7 through Ace.

5. A. This is one hand we play differently depending on the number of decks in play. In the multiple-deck game we defined here, we just hit 11 against an Ace. In a single-deck game, we double down whenever we have 11, even against an Ace.

You're more likely to get a good card on your double-down in a single-deck game than in one using multiple decks. Why? See answer number 14 in *Blackjack Hand Number 4: Good Rules, Bad Rules.*

6. C. Even against a 10, we have an advantage when we start the hand with 11. We want to press that advantage home by doubling down. Sometimes it means we'll lose double our bet, but in the long run we'll win a little less than $180 per $1,000 originally wagered by doubling down. If we just hit, we'll win less than $120 per $1,000 wagered.

When I wrote this in my newspaper column, I received a letter asking if the expected profit was worth the increased risk. The reader pointed out that by doubling down, I was really risking $2,000, and a $180 profit was just 9 percent of the total risked. The player who just hits and wins $120 for a $1,000 risk has a 12 percent profit.

I replied with an example. Let's say you and I are each betting $10 per hand. We both encounter 100 hands in which we have 11 and the dealer shows a 10. Each time, you hit, and I double down. When those 100 hands are over, you have a profit of $120, and I have a profit of $180. Whose position would you rather be in?

Yes, there is risk. The game wouldn't be in the casino if there wasn't risk. Sometimes it will seem like you draw a 2 or a 3 every time you double down. But stick with the percentages. You'll be better off in the long run.

7. B. An easy one. I rarely see anyone hit 16 vs. a 6. Just about everyone seems to know to let the dealer take the risk of busting here.

8. A. This one's a little tougher than number 7. I see players who just hit the wall at 16. They see 16, and decide that's it. No more cards. They both overestimate their own chance of busting, and underestimate the dealer's chance of beating them by making 17 or better.

I spoke with a couple of players about this at a seminar I gave in Rosemont, Illinois, in 1995. They were under the impression that 7 was almost a dealer bust card, that there was enough of a chance the dealer would bust that they weren't about to chance it themselves.

Guess what? When the dealer shows a 7, he has a 74 percent chance of making 17 or better. You can go broke waiting for the dealer to bust in that situation.

9. A. Whenever you stand on 16, you can win only if the dealer busts. Since the dealer busts with 10 face up only about 21 percent of the time, you won't win very much if you stand on 16. Hit 16 whenever the dealer shows a 7 or better. Stand when he shows a 2 through 6.

There is one other possibility. If the casino offers late surrender, your best chance with 16 against a 10 is to surrender half your bet and conserve your resources. Surrender your 16 whenever the dealer shows a 9, 10 or Ace, and surrender 15 against a 10. One exception: if your 16 consists of a pair of 8s, split instead of surrendering.

Your surrenders won't always please other players. I was playing at the Tropicana in Las Vegas not long ago, seated between two young women from Canada who were making their annual gambling trip. I surrendered a 16, and one woman remarked, "I didn't know you can surrender here," and the other asked, "How does that work?" As I explained how and when to surrender, the fellow at third base grumbled, "I suppose it depends on whether you came to *gamble*."

Blackjack is always a gamble, but playing blackjack well is a matter of taking as much of the gamble out of it as you can. Hitting, standing, splitting pairs, doubling down, even surrendering isn't a matter of trusting to luck, of feeling lucky or unlucky. It's a matter of making the best percentage play for the situation, of taking some of the gamble out of it.

10. C. You have an edge when you have 10 vs. the dealer's 9. Use it. Double down.

11. A. 10 vs. 10 is another matter. Assuming the dealer does not have blackjack, 10 vs. 10 is a very slightly positive situation for the player. (You'll actually lose more often than you win if you include the hands that the dealer stops immediately when she has blackjack.) But the player who doubles down and gives up his ability to hit again if he draws a 6 or under turns the hand into one in which the dealer is the favorite.

12. A. Same situation as number 11. Assuming the dealer

does not have blackjack, doubling down takes a slightly favorable situation and turns it into one where you'll lose a little more often than you win.

13. A. See 14.

14. A. When the dealer shows a 7 or higher, he's likely to make his standing total of 17 or better. He'll make it 74 percent of the time when he starts with 7, 76 percent with 8, 77 percent with 9, 79 percent with 10, and 89 percent with an Ace. Unless we also have 17 or better, we'd better hit.

15. A. Many players like to double down with a two-card total of 9. I like to double down on 9 too, but only in the right situations. A hand in which the dealer shows a 2 is not one of them.

We balance two factors when we double down: How likely is the dealer to bust, and if the dealer doesn't bust, how likely is it that our hand can still win? Here, the balance isn't quite right. The dealer busts when starting with a 2 only about 35 percent of the time, and our 9 isn't quite a strong enough starting point to overcome that. Remember, we can't possibly make 21 if we draw only one card to a 9, and to make 20, we have to be lucky enough to pull our Ace. Our most likely good hand is a 19 if we hit a 10, Jack, Queen or King.

Not only that, if we double down we'll wind up with totals of 16 or less about 46 percent of the time. Those hands lose unless the dealer busts. The bottom line is that our 9 vs. a dealer's 2 is a slightly profitable situation: we'll make a little more than $75 per $1,000 wagers if we hit, but that's cut to about $70 per $1,000 originally wagered if we double down.

16. C. Here's where you double down on 9 in a multiple deck game. When the dealer shows a 3, 4, 5 or 6, his bust percentage rises enough that you increase profits in the long run by doubling on 9. It's still not as strong a play as doubling on 10 or 11, but it's a good one.

17. A. I've seen a rash of doubling down in this situation, and it doesn't seem to matter where I'm playing. I've seen it in

Nevada, in the Midwest, in Mississippi. I generally mind my own business when I'm playing unless I'm asked, but after seeing it once too often I asked a gentleman at the Rio in Las Vegas why he was doubling 9 against 7. "I got to figure the dealer for 17, right?" he replied. "So if I get a 10, I win with 19."

It's nice if the hand works that way, but most of the time it won't. Just as in number 15, you have a 46 percent chance of doubling with a card that gives you 11 through 16, a loser unless the dealer busts. Not only that, one time per 13 you'll draw an 8 that gives you a 17. That's a non-winner, too. It could push a dealer's 17, but it can't win unless the dealer busts. Add that up, and you'll see that more than half the time—54 percent, to be precise—you'll wind up with a hand that can't win unless the dealer busts. And the dealer busts when starting with 7 only 26 percent of the time.

You want to double down in that situation? Not me.

18. A. See 18.

19. A. Never double down on 8 in a multiple-deck game. Number 18, with 8 vs. a dealer's 6, is a bit of a close call. If we hit, we win about $12 per $1,000 originally wagered; if we double down, we cut it to a little less than $10 per $1,000.

Just as with 9 vs. 7, I have seen players double on 8 vs. 7. I haven't nosed into their business, but I presume the reasoning is the same—they figure it's their 18 over a dealer's 17. Unfortunately, they're taking a slightly profitable hand if they just hit and turning it into a long-term loser if they double down.

We do sometimes double down on 8 in single-deck games. If you're playing single-deck blackjack, double on 8 when the dealer shows a 5 or a 6.

20 B. See 21.

21. B. With hard 17 or more, always stand regardless of the dealer's up card. And unless you're counting cards, never take insurance.

"Insurance," by the by, is a misnomer. You're really not insuring anything. Your hand will win, lose or push on its own merits regardless of whether you take insurance. Insurance is really a separate bet, a wager that the dealer has blackjack. Just like any bet in the casino, the insurance wager should be weighed on its own merits, and on its merits, it's a bet most players should never make. It's worthwhile only if a third or more of the remaining cards have 10-values, and the only way to know that is if you're a card counter.

Blackjack Hand Number 7: Basic Strategy for Soft Hands

Looking around the casinos, I see soft hands misplayed far more often than hard hands. They're a little bit trickier, and some players seem to have trouble just reading the cards. See how sharp your strategy is for playing soft hands.

1. **Player has soft 16. Dealer shows a 2.**

   A. Hit
   B. Stand
   C. Double down

2. **Player has soft 16. Dealer shows a 6.**

   A. Hit
   B. Stand
   C. Double down

3. **Player has soft 16. Dealer shows an 8.**

   A. Hit
   B. Stand
   C. Double down

4. **Player has soft 17. Dealer shows a 2.**

   A. Hit
   B. Stand
   C. Double down

5. Player has soft 17. Dealer shows a 5.

    A. Hit
    B. Stand
    C. Double down

6. Player has soft 17. Dealer shows a 7.

    A. Hit
    B. Stand
    C. Double down

7. Player has soft 14. Dealer shows a 4.

    A. Hit
    B. Stand
    C. Double down

8. Player has soft 14. Dealer shows a 5.

    A. Hit
    B. Stand
    C. Double down

9. Player has soft 18. Dealer shows a 2.

    A. Hit
    B. Stand
    C. Double down

10. Player has soft 18. Dealer shows a 6.

    A. Hit
    B. Stand
    C. Double down

11. Player has soft 18. Dealer shows an 8.

    A. Hit
    B. Stand
    C. Double down

12. Player has soft 18. Dealer shows a 10.

    A. Hit

B. Stand

C. Double down

13. Player has soft 15. Dealer shows a 2.

A. Hit

B. Stand

C. Double down

14. Player has soft 15. Dealer shows a 6.

A. Hit

B. Stand

C. Double down

15. Player has soft 19. Dealer shows a 6.

A. Hit

B. Stand

C. Double down

16. Player has soft 19. Dealer shows an Ace.

A. Hit

B. Stand

C. Double down

17. Player has soft 13. Dealer shows a 2.

A. Hit

B. Stand

C. Double down

18. Player has soft 13. Dealer shows a 6.

A. Hit

B. Stand

C. Double down

19. Player has soft 20. Dealer shows a 6.

A. Hit

B. Stand

C. Double down

20. Player has soft 20. Dealer shows a 10.

> A. Hit
> B. Stand
> C. Double down

21. Player has soft 21. Dealer shows a 6.

> A. Hit
> B. Stand
> C. Double down

Blackjack Hand Number 7: Basic Strategy for Soft Hands Answers

1. A. See below.

2. C. See below.

3. A. With a total like soft 16, the only question is whether to hit or double down. With a soft total of less than 18, there is no reason to stand.

I ran into a fellow who had no idea what to do with soft 16 one day at Harrah's in Joliet, Illinois. It was a six-deck game with all the players' cards dealt face up. His first two cards were an Ace and a 5, and he flattened his palm to signal that he wanted to stand. The dealer hesitated, and another player said, "You ought to hit that." I jumped in with, "There's nothing you can draw that would hurt that hand." With a resigned shrug, he signalled to hit instead, and drew a 5 for his 21.

We're not going to be that lucky most of the time, but it does serve to illustrate the point: There's nothing you can draw that can hurt many soft hands. With soft 16, what's the worst that could happen? Draw a 10 that leaves you with a hard 16 that can't win unless the dealer busts? Well, your soft 16 already is a hand that can't win unless the dealer busts. Hit, and you just might draw a low card that'll give you a winning hand.

The only question is whether to double down. With soft 16, double down when the dealer's up card is a 4, 5 or 6. Otherwise, just hit. So here, we hit in questions 1 and 3, and double down in number 2. In number 1, when showing a 2, the dealer will make

17 or better 65 percent of the time, and that's just a little too much for us to risk doubling down. And in number 3, with an 8 up, the dealer will make 21 or better 76 percent of the time. The percentages are much more in our favor in number 2. With that 6 up, the dealer will bust 42 percent of the time. We'll make a hand of 17 or better 38 percent of the time and we'll never bust. That's enough to give us a double-down edge.

4. A. See below

5. C. See below

6. A. Soft 17 is one of the hands that separates blackjack players in the know from the pretenders. Players who understand that it's too risky to hit hard 17 and that 17 is a standing total for the dealer have a hard time grasping that with soft 17, they should either hit or double down.

Back in *Good Rules, Bad Rules*, I explained why it's bad for the player when house rules call for the dealer to hit soft 17. Turn that around, and you'll see that it's also bad for the player to stand on soft 17.

Look, 17 is just not a very good hand. It can only win when the dealer busts. Otherwise, the best it can do is tie another 17. With hard 17, the risk of busting is too great, so we stand. But what's the risk of hitting soft 17? That you'll break up a hand that potentially could push if the dealer also winds up with 17?

There are thirteen denominations in a deck of cards. Four of them—King, Queen, Jack and 10—leave us with a 17 that's no worse than where we started. Another four—Ace, 2, 3 and 4—give us better hands that could win even if the dealer makes a standing hand. The other five cards—5, 6, 7, 8 and 9—leave us with totals that can't win unless the dealer busts. That's only a little worse than where we started, and if the dealer shows a 7 through Ace, we can always hit again. Of every thirteen cards, eight leave us either better off or no worse than where we started, and the other five leave us only in a marginally worse position. Again, the main question is whether to double. With soft 17, double when the dealer shows 3, 4, 5 or 6. Otherwise, hit.

7. A. See below.

8. C. Questions 7 and 8 represent the dividing line in how to play soft 14. Double down when the dealer shows a 5 or 6, but hit against everything else. In either case, it's a profitable situation for us, but we'll make a tad more money if we hit soft 14 if we double down against a 4. However, the up card with which the dealer busts most frequently is 5, so with soft 14 against a 5, we'll make more by doubling than by hitting.

9. B. See below.

10. C. See below.

11. B. See below.

12. A. Soft 18 is the trickiest play among soft hands. As you can see from these four examples, sometimes we hit, sometimes we stand, sometimes we double down. It's the only soft total on which all three plays are viable options. Most players stand on soft 18 regardless of the dealer's up card. The hand is misplayed far more often than soft 17—and soft 17 itself is misplayed too often.

In number 12, we have one of the three situations in which we should hit soft 18. We hit whenever the dealer shows a 9, 10 or Ace. With any of those up cards, the dealer will make 19 or better often enough that our soft 18 is a big loser. If the dealer shows a 10 and we stand, we'll lose about $180 per $1,000 wagered. If we hit, we can cut those losses to about $140 per $1,000.

Even most dealers don't understand this play. One night I was playing at the Stardust in Las Vegas. It was a double-deck game, with the cards dealt face down, and I had Ace-7. The dealer's up card was a 10, so I scratched my cards on the table for a hit. The dealer flipped me a 3 face up. Thrilled with my 21, I slid my first two cards under my chips to signal to stand.

I needed that 21. The dealer had a King face down for a 20. But when the dealer turned up my cards, I got a lecture along with my payoff. "That's really a tough play, honey," she said. "It worked this time, but you're going lose a lot of money hitting

18." Other dealers have been less direct. They shake their heads or roll their eyeballs. But it's the right play. Hit soft 18 whenever the dealer has a 9, 10 or Ace.

In number 9, where the dealer shows a 2, and in number 11, when he shows an 8, we just stand. We stand against a 7, where we don't want to break up our chance to win if the dealer has a 10 face down for a 17, or against an 8, where we don't want to botch up a possible push if the dealer has a 10 face down for 18. We also stand against 2 because the dealer doesn't bust often enough to make it profitable for us to double down. That turns around when the dealer shows 3, 4, 5 or 6. Then we double down.

13. A. See below.

14. C. Play soft 15 the same way as soft 16, as discussed in questions 1, 2 and 3 in this section.

This is as good a place as any to add a caution to be sure to read your cards correctly. One morning I was playing a double-deck game, cards dealt face down, at the Fiesta in northwest Las Vegas. The gentleman to my right held his cards well in front of him, though, and I could see as he played. He started with soft 15—an Ace and a 4—then he drew a 3, then another 3. It looked like 21 to me. Incredibly, he signaled for another hit. Even more incredibly, he drew a Queen, and all was well. When the hand was over, I whispered to him, "You know you just hit 21." He smiled and sighed. "I know. I just read it wrong. Lucky it worked out."

We all misread them sometimes, but it happens most often with soft hands. The only answer is to pay attention to what you're doing.

15. B. See below.

16. B. In the multiple-deck game we defined here, we always stand on soft 19, regardless of the dealer's up card. If you happen to be playing single-deck blackjack, a minor adjustment is needed. In single-deck blackjack, you'll gain a little by doubling down on soft 19 when the dealer shows a 6. That's especially true in single-deck games where the dealer hits soft 17. If the dealer stands on all 17s, there's virtually no difference between standing and doubling down.

17. A. See below.

18. C. Strategy for soft 13 is the same as for soft 14, as discussed in questions 7 or 8. Double down when the dealer shows a 5 or 6. Otherwise, just hit.

19. B. See below.

20. B. Always stand on soft 20. It seems barely worth mentioning, but I have seen players double down on soft 20 against 5s and 6s. You can also read soft 20 as a 10, and that looks like a pretty good start for a double. But 10 is nowhere near as good a hand as 20. Don't get greedy—you'll cost yourself money if you double here.

A few years ago, a casino that I'll not embarrass by naming here sent me a press release on its new rules that limited double downs to two-card totals of 9, 10 or 11. It emphasized that these totals included soft 9 and soft 10. I think I was still shaking my head when my wife found me grumbling in my home office half an hour later. "Who do they think they're fooling?" I muttered. "They put a spin on it as if they expect me to encourage my readers to double down and break up 19s and 20s."

Uh-uh. Not then, and not now.

21. B. Double down on blackjack? Nah, nobody would be that greedy, would they?

Some casinos don't allow this play, and I've never actually seen it happen. I've heard about it, though. I was playing in the Tropicana in Las Vegas, and one gentleman started joking about doubling down on a blackjack. The dealer cut in, "You guys are laughing, but I had a guy do it last week. Big player, had a $1,000 bet down. Wouldn't settle for $1,500. Had to try for $2,000. And you know what? He won."

Thanks, but I'll settle for the $1,500.

Blackjack Hand Number 8: Basic Strategy for Splitting Pairs

Splitting pairs can be a great advantage for a player—he can get more money on the table in advantageous situations, and he can sometimes turn a bad hand into a better risk. Allowing the player to split pairs is one of the ways the casino gives back some of the edge it gains by giving the player the first chance to bust. But in order for splitting pairs to be an advantage, the player has to know when to split and when to just play out the hand.

We'll stick with our assumption of a multiple-deck game in which the dealer stands on all 17s. We need a little more information for pair-splitting decisions. In most questions we'll assume the player is allowed to double down after splitting any pair except Aces, but may take only one card on each split Ace. In numbers 16, 19 and 21, we'll change that assumption and not allow the player to double after splits.

See if you know the right times to break up your pairs:

1. **Player has Ace-Ace. Dealer shows 2.**

   A. Hit.
   B. Stand.
   C. Double down.
   D. Split.

2. **Player has Ace-Ace. Dealer shows 10.**

   A. Hit.
   B. Stand.

C. Double down.

D. Split.

3. Player has 10-10. Dealer shows 6.

A. Hit.

B. Stand.

C. Double down.

D. Split.

4. Player has 9-9. Dealer shows 3.

A. Hit.

B. Stand.

C. Double down.

D. Split.

5. Player has 9-9. Dealer shows 7.

A. Hit.

B. Stand.

C. Double down.

D. Split.

6. Player has 9-9. Dealer shows 9.

A. Hit.

B. Stand.

C. Double down.

D. Split.

7. Player has 9-9. Dealer shows 10.

A. Hit.

B. Stand.

C. Double down.

D. Split.

8. Player has 8-8. Dealer shows 8.

A. Hit.

B. Stand.

C. Double down.

D. Split.

9. Player has 8-8. Dealer shows 10.

    A. Hit.

    B. Stand.

    C. Double down.

    D. Split.

10. Player has 7-7. Dealer shows 7.

    A. Hit.

    B. Stand.

    C. Double down.

    D. Split.

11. Player has 6-6. Dealer shows 2.

    A. Hit.

    B. Stand.

    C. Double down.

    D. Split.

12. Player has 6-6. Dealer shows 6.

    A. Hit.

    B. Stand.

    C. Double down.

    D. Split.

13. Player has 5-5. Dealer shows 5.

    A. Hit.

    B. Stand.

    C. Double down.

    D. Split.

14. Player has 5-5. Dealer shows 10.

    A. Hit.

    B. Stand.

    C. Double down.

    D. Split.

15. Player has 4-4. Dealer shows 6.

    A. Hit.

    B. Stand.

    C. Double down.

    D. Split.

16. Player may not double after split. Player has 4-4. Dealer shows 6.

    A. Hit.

    B. Stand.

    C. Double down.

    D. Split.

17. Player has 3-3. Dealer shows 7.

    A. Hit.

    B. Stand.

    C. Double down.

    D. Split.

18. Player has 3-3. Dealer shows 2.

    A. Hit.

    B. Stand.

    C. Double down.

    D. Split.

19. Player may not double after split. Player has 3-3. Dealer shows 2.

    A. Hit.

    B. Stand.

    C. Double down.

    D. Split.

20. Player has 2-2. Dealer shows 3.

    A. Hit.

    B. Stand.

    C. Double down.

    D. Split.

21. Player may not double after split. Player has 2-2. Dealer shows 3.

A. Hit.
B. Stand.
C. Double down.
D. Split.

Blackjack Hand Number 8: Basic Strategy for Splitting Pairs Answers

1. D. See below.

2. D. A few years ago I was taking a course in Las Vegas, and my classmates were employed in the casino industry, but not in the casinos, if you get the difference. There were young marketers, food service managers and safety engineers, even a maritime officer from a riverboat casino.

One night a large group went out to play at Excalibur, and six of us commandeered an empty blackjack table. It quickly became apparent that I was the only one at the table who had played much blackjack, and the others relied on me for advice for the couple of hours we played.

Kirk, to my left, was particularly inquisitive. Dealt a pair of Aces with the dealer showing a 2, he asked me what to do. I replied, "Always split Aces." He did, and got 5 on one Ace and an 8 on the other. Fortunately, the dealer busted, Kirk won both hands and was all smiles.

A while later, he was dealt another pair of Aces, this time with the dealer showing a 10. "Now John," he began, "what about in this situation, when . . ."

Before he could finish, the whole table repeated in chorus, "ALWAYS SPLIT ACES."

He looked at me. "Even in this situation? When he has a 10?"

I just nodded. He split, and drew a face on each Ace. Nice to look like a prophet every once in a while.

It won't always work out that neatly, but any time the dealer does not have blackjack, we have an edge if we split Aces. In some situations, splitting turns a losing situation into a winner in the long run. If we just hit Ace-Ace against a 10, for example, in the long run we will lose a little more than $60 per $1,000 wagered. If we split, we'll win $180 per $1,000 originally wagered instead. There'll be times when we'll draw 2s and 3s on those Aces, and the dealer will make his 17 or better and we'll lose both hands. But in the long run, we'll win more if we split.

3. B. A newspaper colleague once complained that other players got angry with him, and some had even left the table, when he split 10s. "When the dealer shows a 6," he told me, "I have an advantage. And it seems to me that when I have an advantage, I want as much money on the table as I can get."

I told him that I wouldn't walk out on him, nor would I even whine if he split 10s. "Your decisions belong to you," I told him. "In the long run, they don't affect me one way or another. But you shouldn't split 20s."

The player does have an edge with a 10 against a 6. If you had 7-3, you'd double down. But the edge on 10 vs. 6 is nowhere near as large as on 20 vs. 6. Don't get greedy and break up a winning hand.

4. D. See below.

5. B. See below

6. D. See below.

7. B. The trickiest pair-splitting hand is 9-9. Its total of 18 is on the cusp of being a winning hand, the average winner being a little over 18. Still, 9 is a strong enough building block that we split the pair whenever the dealer shows a 2, 3, 4, 5 or 6. In question number 4, where the dealer shows a 3, we have an advantage we want to press it home by getting our money on the table by splitting the pair.

As good a building block as 9 is, though, it's not strong

enough to break up the 18 when the dealer shows a 7, as in number 5. If the dealer has a 10 face down, which will happen about 30.8 percent of the time, our 18 beats his 17. If he has an Ace down, then our 18 ties his 18. And we'll win enough of the remaining hands that we have a larger edge by standing on 18 against a 7 than if we split the pair.

The situation reverses itself when the dealer shows an 8 or a 9. With an 8, if the dealer has a 10 down he ties our 18, and if he has an Ace he beats us—obviously a tougher situation for the player than if the dealer wins a 7. We'll win often enough when the dealer has other cards face down that we have a slight edge overall if we stand on 9-9 vs. an 8. But we more than double that edge if we split 9-9. (We slightly less than double our edge by splitting if doubling down after splits is not allowed.)

With 9-9 vs. 9, as in number 6, we're cutting our losses instead of pressing our advantage. Now if we stand, we lose whenever the dealer has a 10 down, and tie if he has a 9. (If he has an Ace down, he has blackjack. In most American casinos, we lose before we have a chance to split.) That's too big an edge to overcome, but we can cut our losses nearly in half if we split.

When the dealer shows a 10, as in number 7, or an Ace, we can't even cut our losses. Against the dealer's best up cards, we'll lose both hands too often to split. Better to stand on 18 and be grateful for the occasions that it wins.

So with 9-9, split when the dealer shows 2 through 6, stand against a 7, split against 8 or 9, and stand against 10 or Ace.

8. D. See below.

9. D. On the list of the most frequently misplayed hands in blackjack, number 9 ranks near the top. Most players worry too much about the dealer having a 10 face down, meaning that by splitting they've most likely created two losing hands instead of one.

Hey, it happens. A lot. I remember playing at Harrah's Northern Star in Joliet, Illinois, when it first opened. Before more casinos were built, the first Midwestern riverboats were always crowded. If you had a seat at the table, you could count on three or four would-be players standing at your shoulder. I split 8s against a 10, and drew a face card on each for two 18s. A woman at my shoulder, enthused, "Oh, good for you. Nice hit." I grimaced and waited for what every player really expects in that situation: the dealer turned over a 10 for a 20 to take both hands.

Splitting 8s against a 10 is not a winning play. It is a DEFENSIVE play. Look back at number 7, and note that one of the reasons we stand with 9-9 against 10 is that 18 will win often enough when the dealer doesn't have a 10 down that we lose less by standing than by splitting. That's not so with 8-8—16 is a TERRIBLE hand. If we stand, we can't win unless the dealer busts, which isn't going to happen very often when he starts with 10. If we hit, we have a big risk of busting and we win only slightly more often.

We have better building blocks if we start each hand with 8. Starting with an 8 vs. a 10 is not a winning situation, but it's a darn sight better than starting with 16. We will lose less money in the long run if we split the 8s than if we hit or stand.

Splitting 8s against a 7, as in number 8, is an OFFENSIVE play, and a really good one. Here, we take a hand that is a long-term loser and turn it into a long-term winner. Stand on 16 vs. 7, and lose about $480 per $1,000 wagered. Hit, and lose about $410 per $1,000. But split, and in the long run the expected result is a profit of nearly $220 per $1,000 if double downs are permitted after splits, and about $170 per $1,000 if doubles after splits are not allowed.

Whether for offensive or defensive reasons, splitting 8s is always a good play.

10. D. It's far better to split the 7s than to play a 14 against a 7. You want to be in the position that if the dealer has a 10 down, you'll push if you're dealt a 10. If you're dealt that 10 on top of a 14, you bust and lose regardless of what the dealer has down. That's a bit of an oversimplification, but you'll cut your losses from about $410 per $1,000 if you hit to less than $90 per $1,000 if you split.

When I mentioned this in my newspaper column, a reader

asked why split 7s still lost a little to a dealer's 7 in the long run. After all, she asked, it's an even situation, isn't it? Your 7 against the dealer's 7? Should the long-term results be even?

The dealer has an edge with 7 up vs. your 7 for the same reason the house has an edge on the game of blackjack. The player has the first chance to bust, and if both player and dealer bust, the house wins.

11. D. See below.

12. D. When the dealer shows a 2, as in number 11, splitting 6-6 is a borderline call. A common variation in table rules makes all the difference. If you are permitted to double down after splits, it'll cut your losses a little to split the pair. If you are not permitted to double after splits, just play the hand as a 12, and hit when the dealer has a 2.

Playing 6-6 when the dealer shows a 6, as in number 12, is an interesting little hand. Here, we turn a losing hand into one that makes a little money in the long run by splitting the 6s if we're allowed to double after splits. If we're not, then splitting the 6s just cuts our losses. Either way, we split 6s against a 6.

Here, we defined a game in which we are permitted to double after splits, so we split in both 11 and 12. Overall, split 6s when the dealer's up card is 2 through 6 if you're allowed to double after splits; if not, just split when the dealer shows 3 through 6.

13. C. See below.

14. A. Never split 5s. A 10 is a much stronger building block than a 5. With a 10, a one card draw can give us 20 (with a 10, Jack, Queen or King) or 21 (with an Ace). Eight of 13 possible one-card draws give us 17 or better. There are no one-card draws that can turn a 5 into 17 or better. Without at least two draws, 5 can't turn into anything that wins, or even pushes, without the dealer busting.

Just as with any other 10, the question becomes whether to double down. Double when the dealer shows 2 through 9, but just hit when the dealer's up card is a 10-value card or an Ace.

Following those rules, we double down in number 13, where the dealer shows a 5, but just hit against the 10 in number 14.

Incidentally, 5s are the only pair with which we double down before splitting. When you push out a second bet, the dealer will want to make sure you're doubling and not splitting. Usually they'll ask verbally, "One card?" If you reply simply, "One card," they'll know you're doubling and not splitting.

The assumption is that doubling is the more common play as well as the right one, but the dealer has to check to make sure. Only once have I seen the assumption go the other way. At the Horseshoe in Tunica County, Mississippi, the first baseman pushed out a second bet on his pair of 5s, and before the poor player knew what was happening, the dealer split them up and dealt a 10 on the first one.

"No! I wanted to double down, not split," the fellow shouted.

The dealer had to call over the pit boss, who shrugged, put the 5s back together and gave the fellow the 10 for his 20. And the first baseman won his double down.

15. D. See below.

16. A. When the player is not permitted to double after splits, splitting 4s is always a bad play. In the case of 4-4 against a 6, the player has an edge. Splitting when not allowed to double after splits waters down that edge, but splitting when we can follow by doubling down enhances the edge. If we draw a 5, 6 or 7 on top of a split 4 so that we have 9, 10 or 11 against a 6, we want to be able to double down.

So here, we split in number 15, when we are allowed to double after splits, and just hit in number 16, when we are not.

The distinction led to my being lectured one day at a book signing at Harrah's in Joliet, Illinois. One gentleman thumbed through a copy of my *Gaming: Crusing the Casinos With Syndicated Gambling Columnist John Grochowski*. He looked me in the eye and said, "I don't agree with your book."

I smiled and replied, "OK, what did I mess up?"

"You don't just hit 4s against a 6," he answered, "You split."

I pointed out that he was looking at a section on splitting pairs when not allowed to double after splits, then showed him the distinction in a later section on splitting when doubling after splits is permitted. He nodded, put the book down and headed for the riverboat. No sale, but at least I had a satisfied non-customer.

17. D. See below.

18. D. See below.

19. A. When I watch other players try to decide what to do with 3-3, the most common decisions seem to be to split when the dealer's up card is a 5 or 6, hem and haw when the dealer shows a 2, 3 or 4, and just hit when the dealer shows a 7 or higher. But 6 is not a very good starting hand. We'll actually save ourselves a little money if we split 3s against a 7, as in number 17. Splitting doesn't turn the hand into a winner, but it loses less money in the long run. Also, always split 3s if the dealer shows a 4, 5 or 6. It becomes a borderline decision when the dealer's up card is a 2, as in number 18 and number 19, or a 3. In number 18, we're allowed to double down after splitting the pair, so we split. In number 19, there's no doubling after splits, so we just hit.

20. D. See below.

21. A. Play 2-2 the same way as 3-3: split against 4 through 7, hit against 8 through Ace, and check the rules when the dealer shows a 2 or a 3. In number 20, we can double after splits, so we split. We just hit in number 21 when doubling after splits is not allowed.

Splitting is not risk free, even if it is to our advantage when we can double afterward. Sometimes we'll lose both bets—or even more. Once at the Tropicana in Las Vegas, I split 2s against a 2, then received another 2 and split again. On my first 2, I was then dealt a 9, so I doubled down, and got an Ace. So on hand number 1, I was stuck with total of 12. On number 2, I received a King, then a Jack. I busted. On number 3, I drew a 4, then a 6 for 12, then another Jack. Busted again.

The two other gentlemen at the table shook there heads and one said softly, "Now that THAT mess is cleared up . . ."

Soon afterward, the dealer cleared up the rest of the mess. She made 18, beating my 12 with the double down bet. I lost four bets on the hand—and it's never fun when that happens. But that's blackjack. All you can do is play with the percentages and know that next time, splitting the pair is still the best play to make.

Blackjack Hand Number 9: Keeping Count

If you have all the strategy discussed in the last three hands down pat, you're ready to play the casino almost even. But are you ready to take the edge?

This little true-or-false quiz is by no means the last word in counting cards. If you want a complete primer on card counting, check out one of the many excellent works on blackjack listed in the bibliography at the end of this book. But check out the answers here to see how much you already know.

1. **Card counters memorize every card as it is played.**

   True
   False

2. **Proficient card counters still lose more hands than they win.**

   True
   False

3. **The card counter has an edge because he has an idea what cards are most likely to come next, and can change his playing strategy to fit the situations.**

   True
   False

4. **The most important element in counting cards is the balance between high cards and low cards remaining to be played.**

    True
    False

5. **The card counter raises his bets when the count tells him the dealer is most likely to bust.**

    True
    False

6. **Counts favorable to the player occur less frequently in multiple-deck games than in single-deck games.**

    True
    False

7. **Counting cards is cheating.**

    True
    False

8. **Players have used hidden computers to help keep count.**

    True
    False

9. **Most card counters pose no real threat to the casino.**

    True
    False

10. **All players at a table benefit when one good card counter is at the table.**

    True
    False

Blackjack Hand Number 9: Keeping Count Answers

1. False. I've had a number of readers tell me, "You must have to be like Dustin Hoffman in *The Rain Man* to count cards with six or eight decks." That's not the case; the counter isn't trying to memorize every card. At a given moment, he couldn't tell you how many 4s or 8s or Jacks have been played. Instead, nearly all counters use plus-minus system, in which they need keep only one number in their heads from hand to hand.

There are many card counting systems. One of the most commonly used is called the Hi-Lo. Each card is assigned a value—Aces, Kings, Queens, Jacks and 10s are minus-1, while 2s, 3s, 4s, 5s and 6s are plus-1. That leaves 7s, 8s and 9s with a value of zero.

As you see cards, you add and subtract their values in your head to keep a running count. For example, you're dealt a King and a Queen. The dealer has a 6 face up. At this point, the count is minus-1 for your king, another minus-1 for your Queen and plus-1 for the dealer's 6, leaving a total of minus-1. The dealer turns up a 7, then pulls a 4 for 17. The 7 is a zero card so you ignore it in the running count. The four is plus-1, leaving the overall count for the hand at zero.

Counting with a plus-minus system like this is not difficult, but it does take practice and concentration. Practicing at home, whether on a computer or with decks of cards, is essential. If you can't keep an accurate count at home when it's quiet and you can play at your own pace, you'll never pull it off in a casino where the dealer is trying to push the cards out as fast as she can, the lights are flashing, slots and players provide a constant background din and the cocktail waitress is at your elbow wondering if you need a drink. And keeping accurate count is just the beginning of the battle. We'll look at some other steps in more answers in this section.

2. True. The same house edge that works against everyone else is still in force against card counters—the player has the first chance to go bust, and if both player and dealer bust, the house wins.

Card counters can narrow the gap a little by making adjustments in basic strategy according to the count, but they can't totally overcome it to the point they win more hands than the dealer.

Look at it this way: counters do well to gain an edge over the house of 1 percent or so. We've already seen that the house gives 2.3 percent back to the player when it pays 3-2 on blackjacks. If the player could win as many hands as the dealer, he'd have a 2.3 percent edge just because of blackjack payoffs. The counter's edge doesn't come from winning more hands; it comes from recognizing the right times to have larger-than-usual bets on the table.

3. False. The card counter DOESN'T know which card is likely to come next. All he knows is whether more high cards (those with minus-1 values in the Hi-Lo system) have been played, or whether more low cards (with plus-1 values) have been dealt. Some strategy adjustments are made depending on that count, but they are far less important than adjusting bet size in accordance with the count.

Neither the strategy nor bet size adjustments are made strictly according to the running count we discussed in number 1. First, the player must normalize the count to the number of decks remaining in play. That's called the "true count." For example, if we have a running count of plus-12, that means 12 more low cards than high cards already have been played. If we're midway through a six-deck shoe, with three decks yet unseen, we divide that running count of plus-12 by the three remaining decks to get a true count of plus-4. That true count tells us what strategy adjustments we should make. If the count is negative, that means more high cards have been dealt, there's a higher-than-usual concentration of low cards remaining. If the count is positive, then more low cards have been dealt and there's a high concentration of high cards remaining. These changes make it advantageous to make the following strategy adjustments:

- True count of minus 1 or less: Hit 13 when the dealer shows a 2 or 3. Hit 12 against a 4, 5 or 6.
- True count of 0 or plus 1: Use normal basic strategy.
- True count of plus 2 or more: Double down on 11 against an Ace; double down on 8 against a 6; stand on 12 against a 3; stand on 16 against a 10 if your 16 is made up of three or more cards.
- True count of plus 3 or more: Always take insurance; stand on 12 against a 2; double down on 10 against an Ace, on 9 against a 2 and 8 against a 5.

If you're well-versed in basic strategy, some of this will go against the grain. Sometimes you might even get static from other players. I did one day at Treasure Island in Las Vegas. With a big positive true count, I stood on a four-card 16 against a 10. One talky fellow asked, "Don't you hit 16s against 10s?"

"Usually," I replied.

"Usually?" he pressed his point. "When don't you? When is it not the right play to hit that hand?"

I just shrugged it off. The last thing you want to do is say, "Hey, we have a true count of plus-5 here and I'm so likely to bust that I can't hit 16." The pit crew takes a dim view of players even thinking such things, much less blurting them out. So I kept quiet.

The next shoe was uneventful. The count never strayed far above or below zero, and I didn't need to make any more unorthodox plays. Everyone at the table seemed to be playing basic strategy. After a while, the other fellow said, "That's what I like. A whole table, everyone playing by the book." Every few hands he'd comment again on "playing by the book," until he left after about an hour. As he cleared earshot, another player grumbled, "I'd like to take that book and hit him with it."

I just smiled.

4. True. The basic concept behind counting cards is that high cards tend to favor the player and low cards favor the dealer.

Why? First, because there are more blackjacks, which pay the player 3-2, when there is a high concentration of high cards remaining to be dealt. Also, in double down situations, the player is more likely to get the high card he needs when more high cards are remaining. When there are a lot of low cards left, the dealer is more likely to pull out one of those miracle multi-card 21s that so frustrate players. It doesn't work both ways, either. If you get to 16 and the dealer shows a 6, you stand. If the dealer then has 16, he must hit, and if there's a high concentration of low cards remaining, he's more likely to draw a little one to beat you.

The bottom line is that negative counts, which mean more high cards than low cards already have been played, favor the dealer. Positive counts, with more high cards as yet undealt, favor the player.

5. False. Counters raise their bets when blackjacks are most likely to occur. The biggest gain to be made by counting cards comes from having more money on the table when the cards remaining to be played increase the likelihood of two-card 21s being dealt. Bets are kept small when there's a negative count that favors the dealer. But the bigger the positive count, the more money the player wants on the table.

Beginners might try a simple 1-to-5 betting spread. When the count is negative or neutral, bet one unit. With a true count of plus-1, bet two units; at plus-2, bet three units and at plus-3 or more, bet five units. Your betting unit can be anything. If your basic bet at neutral counts is $5 per hand, then with a 1-to-5 spread, you're betting from $5 to $25 per hand.

Experienced counters will want to get a larger spread than that whenever they can. If you find you can spread 1-to-10 without getting hassled by the pit, so much the better. Then you might start with a two-unit bet at neutral counts, drop to one unit in negative counts, but increase to four at plus-1, six at plus-2, eight at plus-3 and 10 at plus-4 or more. One colleague of mine tries to push to a 1-to-20 spread.

It's not as simple as saying, "Oh, today I'm going to spread 1-to-20." The casino has something to say about that. Casinos that are on the lookout for card counters watch for the bet spread first. Most players who vary their bets from hand-to-hand are playing hunches or betting progressions, but if the casino detects that the player's betting pattern fits their profile for a card counter, they'll give his play a closer look, then eventually take action. The casino might start shuffling early, or limiting the player's bet size, or even bar the counter from playing.

Some casinos will tolerate bigger spreads than others. There are two on my regular rounds that are at opposite ends of the spectrum. At one, I have no trouble getting a 1-to-12 spread. I've never been hassled in this casino. At the other, the pit crew gets antsy if I use the beginner's 1-to-5 spread. Coincidentally, the casino that doesn't worry as much about counters also has better table rules. I know for certain that one of the executives in the operation is a card counter himself—I've seen him play elsewhere. My guess is that the powers that be at that casino decided that they make so much money off average players that a few counters are little bother, and that it's good for business when others see a player winning.

Every casino has its breaking point, though. Even the tolerant ones will take action if your maximum bets are large enough that you're costing them serious money. Every counter must develop a sense for the casino's breaking point. Keep your spreads under the point where the casino feels it must take action. In the case of the house that panics even at 1-to-5, well, I usually stay away from its blackjack tables.

6. True. The effect of removing one card of fifty-two from play in single-deck blackjack is much larger than the effect of removing one of 312 from play in a six-deck game. If you have a running count of plus-4—easily attainable in a single hand—you're in great position in a single-deck game. But let's say it's a six-deck game and there are still four unseen decks. Now your true count is only plus-1—not bad, but not a count that has you wanting to push your maximum bet out.

Multiple-deck blackjack often is a waiting game for counters. I've gone whole shoes, even a couple of shoes at a time, making minimum bets because the favorable counts never came. There are quicker, wider swings in the true count when fewer decks are used.

That doesn't mean single-deck games are easier to count. They're not. It's just as easy to keep a plus/minus figure in your head from hand to hand with six decks in play as with one. Not only that, most multiple-deck games are dealt face up, making it easier to see all the cards than in face-down single-deck games. However, some card counters gravitate to the single-deck games because the more variable true count means favorable situations occur much more frequently than in multiple-deck games.

7. False. Counting cards is skillful play, not cheating. It is not illegal in any jurisdiction in the United States. The casinos don't want you to have the edge, and they can take measures against you if they think you have the edge, but gaining an edge by skillful play is not cheating.

Not long ago I wrote a series on counting cards in my newspaper column. A copy editor who read my columns before they appeared in print came to my desk. "I don't gamble, but that was fascinating," she told me. "And what I found most fascinating of all was that we can publish it. Are we allowed to show people how to do that?"

Yes, we are. Counting cards only has to be kept secret when you do it in a casino, and even then only because we don't want the casino to toughen playing conditions or bar us from playing.

8. True, although it's no longer legal to use electronic devices to help win at casino games.

The late Ken Uston for a time used a concealed computer as detailed in his book, *Million Dollar Blackjack*. The operator used his toes to push buttons and key in cards as they appeared. Uston and his associated used the computer right up until the time laws barring electronic aids to casino players went into effect.

Uston also pioneered team play, a practice that continues today and which is a far greater threat to casino profits than any individual counter. Typically, a card counter making table minimum bets waits for a favorable situation, then gives a signal for a non-counting "big player" to sit down. Since he plays only when signalled by the counter that the time is right, the big player bets only in favorable situations—he never bets when the house has an edge. And since he's not responsible for counting cards, he can play the high roller, have a good time, have a few drinks, even milk the casino for big-ticket comps.

With a counter and big player teaming up, the bet spread can be much larger than 1-to-10 or 1-to-20. Let's say the casino has a $5 minimum bet and a $500 maximum. The counter bets $5 per hand; when signalled, the big player bets $500 until time to leave the table. That's a 1-to-100 spread that's much more dangerous to the casino than anything a single player can do.

9. True. Most players who try to count cards don't do it very well. They might find they can't keep count under casino conditions, or they have trouble estimating the number of decks left to play and can't make the conversion to the true count. Others might have difficulty applying the true count to bet size or strategy adjustments.

Even a good counter can't do much damage if he's underfinanced. To get a 1-to-10 spread, a player at a $5 minimum table must be prepared for situations in which he should bet $50. You can't sit down at a $5 table with $100 and expect to be successful counting cards. Better to have at least $500 to $1,000 for a session of counting cards with $5 minimum bets. And if you're prepared to risk that much money, you'd better be prepared to lose it, because sometimes the house wins, even when you have an edge. If it's the dealer who keeps getting blackjack in positive counts, you can console yourself with the thought that yours pay

3-2 if they ever come, but the bottom line is that it's still a losing session.

Most would-be counters are missing at least one piece of the puzzle—knowledge, discipline, practice or bankroll. Some might play the casino even, some might make a little bit of money, but nothing that really hurts the casino. It's the few who have all the pieces in place the casino really has to worry about.

10. False. I received a letter not long ago that asked if the others at a table benefitted from having a counter play. Unfortunately, they do not. There is nothing magical about having the cards counted that benefits everyone. The counter benefits mostly from having bigger bets on the table in favorable situations, and partly from being able to adjust hit/stand decisions according to the count. The only way a non-counter at the table could benefit from the counter's actions would be if he knew what the counter was doing, and raised and lowered his own bets at the same time.

Blackjack Hand Number 10: Life's Little Oddities

I once received a letter from a woman who wondered why the reds on hearts and diamonds in casino decks seemed to be a deeper shade than in the cards she has at home. I dutifully phoned a table games manager and was told, "Yeah, I guess they aren't as bright a red as a deck you'd buy in the store. There's no reason for it. It's just the trend."

The ten true or false questions that follow all are adapted from my mail. They cover anything from casino procedures to games based on blackjack to casino comps. See if these answers fit your experience in the casinos.

1. **Once bets are settled and the dealer moves to the next hand, results are final.**

    True.
    False.

2. **New decks of cards are put in play only at the beginning of each shift.**

    True.
    False.

3. **It is to the house's advantage to have automatic shufflers.**

    True.
    False.

4. The player options offered in Spanish 21 prove most casinos have blackjack games that are too tough. (Note: Spanish 21 pays big bonuses on hands of 7-7-7 and it has many rules favorable to the player, among them the ability to double down on three cards and "rescue" his double down by surrendering only his original bet if he draws a bad card.)

> True.
> False.

5. In Multiple-Action blackjack, the player should adjust strategy so he never busts. (Note: In Multiple-Action 21, the player gets one hand, but may make three bets. The dealer gets one up card, but then uses it to start three different hands, one for each wager. If the player busts, he loses all three bets. But if he stands, he has three chances at the dealer busting.)

> True.
> False.

6. Tournaments in which no-value funny money is used and in which all entry fees are returned as prize money are better for the player than tournaments that use real money.

> True.
> False.

7. In tournament play, the player's best chance is to hoard his money, make small bets and let the house edge work against the other players.

> True.
> False.

8. Players who don't want to count cards can gain an edge by playing solid basic strategy and using a progressive betting system.

> True.
> False.

9. **Blackjack players who wager $5 a hand or more should expect a complimentary dinner buffet after a couple of hours of play.**

   True.
   False.

10. **The casino will give comps to players regardless of whether they win or lose.**

   True.
   False.

Blackjack Hand Number 10: Life's Little Oddities Answers

1. False. It seems like it should be that way, and most casinos won't bother you if the dealer's made a mistake and paid you on a hand you didn't really win. But that can be affected by anything from state regulations to the shift manager's paranoia about the bottom line.

The expansion of gaming across the nation has led to little inconsistencies from state to state. In some jurisdictions, casinos are required by law to recover any money paid to a player by mistake. That's typical in riverboat states where state gaming taxes hover around 20 percent of adjusted gross receipts and range up to 35 percent on the most successful casinos in Illinois. That compares with gaming taxes of about 6 percent in Nevada and 8 percent in Mississippi. With such a high proportion of every bet belonging to the state, government wants to make darn sure it gets its share.

That leads to some really uncomfortable situations. One reader told me she'd been tracked down at a slot machine and told by a casino employee that the surveillance cameras had caught a mistake at a blackjack table, that she'd been overpaid by $10. The casino wanted the money back. "I don't recall being overpaid," she said. "And I don't think I should give back any money." The casino employee's response: "Then we can have you arrested when the boat docks."

Contrast that with an experience I had at Excalibur on the Las Vegas Strip. I'd lost several hands in a row, and had a 17 with the dealer showing a 9. When everyone had completed play, the dealer turned up an 8—he also had a 17. But when he got to me, he didn't knock the table to indicate a push and move on. He looked me square in the eye and paid me. He knew exactly what he was doing.

Same table, about 20 minutes later, with the dealer showing an 8, the woman at first base had a 16. In the next seat, I had an 11 and already had extra chips on the table to double down. The woman signalled to stand, but the dealer gave her a card any-way—the 10 I needed for my 21, but which busted the woman's hand. I received a useless 4 on my double down.

The woman protested that she didn't want a card, so the dealer called over the pit boss. He picked up the 10.

"You don't want this card?" he asked the woman.

"No, I don't," she said flatly.

The pit boss turned to me. "*You* want this card."

I smiled. "I sure do," I replied.

He buried the 4 in the discard tray and gave me the 10. When the dealer turned up a 10 for 18, the woman at first base lost, but I won my double down.

I've heard similar stories from other regions. One friend of mine tells of playing in Mississippi and rolling his eyeballs when he received a 16 against a dealer's 10. "Don't worry," the pit boss told him. "You're going to win this hand." When my friend hit and drew a 10, the pit boss discarded it and told the dealer to give him another card. That one was an 8, and it was discarded, as was the 10 that followed. Finally a 5 came out, and just as the pit boss had promised, my friend won the hand.

Such moves don't really cost the casino—or the state—much money. It's not as if most players put extra chips away and walk out of the casino with the money. Most of them replay their chips and the casino winds up winning the same amount they would have without any extra payoff. But the customer feels like he's gotten a little extra for his money, and he feels good about the ex-perience. That's a 180-degree turn from the ill will created when a casino tries to recover mistake payouts long after the fact.

Threatening a customer with arrest because of a casino mistake should never happen, but it does.

2. False. Practices vary from casino to casino. With six-deck or eight-deck shoes, some change cards at the beginning of each shift, some change as infrequently as once per day.

Cards are changed much more frequently at single-deck and double-deck games. Fewer decks means the cards have to be shuffled more frequently, increasing wear, tear and the likelihood that cards will be bent. I played a long session of double-deck one night in a casino that changed cards once every two hours. Others leave cards in play a little longer than that, but any casino dealing blackjack from one or two decks changes cards at least a couple of times per shift.

3. True, but not because automatic shufflers mix the cards differently or make it any less likely the player will win. Automatic shufflers favor the house because more hands per hour are played when the dealer doesn't have to stop to shuffle the cards.

At a full seven-player table, an average of about 50 hands per hour are played. Let's say two players are each betting $10 per hand, risking $500 per hour. One is an average player facing a house edge of about 2 percent. His average expected losses come to about $10 per hour. The other is a basic strategy player, facing a house edge of about half a percent. His average expected losses come to about $2.50 per hour. Let's say the casino introduces automatic shufflers, and this full table is averaging 60 hands per hour. Now our $10 bettors are risking $600 per hour instead. The average player's expected hourly losses rise to $12 per hour. The basic strategy player's average expected losses rise to $3 per hour.

Does anyone besides the casino benefit from automatic shufflers? Yes. Increasing the number of hands per hour benefits whoever has the edge in a game. In most cases, that's the casino. But there are a few players who turn the tables and take an edge over the house in blackjack, so these card counters benefit from automatic shufflers.

4. False. To go with all its plusses, Spanish 21 has one big negative. All the 10-spot cards are removed from play. The game uses six 48-card decks with no 10s. There are still Kings, Queens and Jacks, but with no 10s, there are fewer blackjacks and good cards on double downs are tougher to come by.

Spanish 21 is a fun game, and not a bad one for a player who studies it and makes basic strategy adjustments to account for all the oddball rules along with there being no 10s. Against a basic strategy player, the house has an edge of about 0.7 percent, compared with 0.5 percent in a typical six-deck blackjack game.

5. False. The same basic strategy that helps cut the house edge in regular blackjack should be used in Multiple Action. The player who stands on 16 when the dealer shows a 7 in Multiple Action is giving his money away just as surely as the player who stands on 16 vs. 7 in regular blackjack. A 16 can't win unless the dealer busts, and when he starts with a 7 he's only going to bust 26 percent of the time. That remains the same no matter how many times he uses that 7 to start a new hand. The player has a better shot at winning if he hits 16 against 7, no matter how many bets are on the table.

Players who cannot stand to bust and see the dealer scoop up three bets at once shouldn't play Multiple Action.

6. True. A tournament in which no money changes hands at the tables and all entry fees are returned to the players as prize money is called a "100 percent equity tournament." The casino makes no money off the tournament itself. In fact, it costs the casino a little money for its administrative costs as well as any free T-shirts, rooms or meals that are included with entry. Casinos that run such tournaments figure they make any losses back in customer goodwill, as well as from the customers playing regular games when not in their tournament rounds.

Sometimes tournaments are organized such that all entry fees are returned to players as prize money, but require that live money be used during tournament play. Casinos that run such tournaments usually emphasize that players keep all winnings during tournament play. That sounds attractive to players who have had a hot hand in a funny-money tournament, winning hundreds or even thousands of dollars in a round, and keeping none of it.

But when live money is used, players are bucking the usual house edge—the casino can make back its cost of running the event just from normal player losses during tournament play. In fact, the house edge is magnified because sometimes tournament players are forced to make bad plays.

Let's say you're on the last hand in a tournament semifinal. One player from your table advances to the finals, and only players in the finals receive prize money. You are in second place with $700, and the leader has $1,290. The leader bets ahead of you, and makes a table minimum wager of $5. You're normally just a $25 bettor, but you bet the table maximum of $300. At this point, you can't catch up unless you double down or split a pair. If you win and the leader loses, you have $1,000 and he has $1,285. Even a blackjack gives you only $1,150.

The cards are dealt, and you have a 16 against the dealer's 10. What to do? The only way to reach the finals is to double down, but it's a terrible situation, a hand you're going to lose more than 75 percent of the time. If there's enough prize money involved, you have to go for it. So a bettor who normally risks only $25 at a time finds himself risking $600 with a relatively small chance of winning. When there's live money on the table, the house is the beneficiary in the long run.

7. False. There are many different ways to approach a tournament round. Some players like to bet big early, hoping to get lucky at the beginning and force the other players to chase them. Others make minimum bets for a while, hope attrition takes care of a few other players at the table, then bet big when they know who the contenders are. Any successful tournament strategy, though, relies at getting your money on the table at some point. Betting small and breaking even isn't going to get it done most of the time.

8. False. I've had an interesting discussion off and on with Walter Thomason, author of *The Ultimate Blackjack Book* and editor of *The Experts' Guide to Casino Games*, in which I contributed the blackjack chapter as well as an overview of the history of gaming in the United States. Walter is a progression player who increases his bets when he wins and decreases his bets when he loses. He'd been on quite a winning streak when we exchanged phone calls and faxes over the spring and summer of 1997. Walter contends that the mathematicians are wrong and that a betting progression can overcome the house's mathematical edge. I remain doubtful.

I have nothing against betting progressions. They can be fun, and for a non-card counter they can sometimes yield spectacular results. I once watched a progression player at the Tropicana in Las Vegas start with $5 bets and win $345 in 45 minutes. There's no way he could have matched that betting a flat $5 a hand.

The flip side is that betting progressions lead to more frequent losses. That's because losses inevitably come with a bigger bet on the table. Let's take the progression I watched the fellow play at the Trop. He started with a $5 bet, and any time he lost he went back to $5. If he won he bet $5 again, but then if he won again he bet $10, then $10, $15, $15, $25 and $25. It took two winning bets at each level to move up. That makes some sense, because it means that any time the player wins two bets in a row he can do no worse than break even for the sequence. If he advanced his bet after each win, he could lose money on sequences starting with a win—for example, a $5 win followed by a $10 loss is a net $10 loss.

Still, compare what happens when two wins are followed by a loss. If the player wins $5 and $5 and follows with a $10 loss, he's back to even. If he were flat-betting $5 a hand instead, he'd win $5 and $5, then lose $5 and still have $5 in profits. If he then loses the next hand starting a new sequence, the flat bettor is back to even, while the progression bettor now has $5 in losses after winning two bets and losing two. Perfectly normal sequences like that mean progression bettors will sustain small losing sessions more frequently than flat bettors, balancing off the occasional big wins.

One other question no progression bettor has been able to answer for me. By raising bets after a win or a couple of wins, the progression player is saying that the likelihood is that he's going to keep winning. Just what is it about past wins that makes future wins more likely? If I've won two bets in a row and the gentleman next to me has lost two in a row, progression systems say I should raise my bet while he should lower his. What makes me more likely to win and him more likely to lose on the same hand? I'm not trying to dissuade anyone from trying progressions—they're fun and a heck of a lot less work than counting cards. But I don't see them as a surefire way to beat the casinos, either.

9. False. The rise of slot clubs in the 1980s and '90s has left some table players wondering if they're the second-class citizens nowadays. One fellow wrote to me to complain that his wife, a quarter slot player, is always getting meal comps and free coin offers in the mail, while he, a $5 blackjack player, gets nothing.

The plain fact is that slot players are more valuable to the casino than low-limit blackjack players. Let's say you're playing blackjack at $5 per hand, 50 hands per hour, and the house figures it has a 2 percent edge over an average player. You're betting $250 per hour, and the house assumes that on the average, it's going to win $5 per hour from you. (That's a fair rule of thumb. The house figures it's going to win one of your average bets per hour. Sometimes you'll win, sometimes you'll lose a lot more than the average, but in the long run it balances out to one bet per hour.)

How much of that will it kick back in the form of comps? Anywhere from 10 percent to 40 percent of your expected loss, depending on individual casino policies and competitive pressures. You can expect a lot higher comp rate in downtown Las Vegas than Native American casino with no competitor for 100 miles around.

At a 20 percent comp rate, your $5 bets are worth about $1 per hour in comps. You're going to have to put in an eight-hour shift at the tables just to earn a buffet comp for one. Some casinos with plenty of higher-rolling players won't even bother rating your play for comps at that level.

Now let's take a quarter slot player, wagering three quarters

per pull. Most newer slot machines are equipped with bill validators, so the player can just slide in a $20 bill and have 80 credits
pop up on a quarter machine. The player doesn't go through the
time consuming process of feeding quarters into a slot, then
pulling the handle. With credits on the screen, it's just push the
button and spin, push the button and spin. It's easy to get in 500
pulls per hour on machines with bill validators. Under tournament conditions, when the object for slot players is just to set the
reels spinning as often as possible in the alloted time, I've seen
players clocked at more than 900 spins per hour.

At 500 pulls per hour and 75 cents per pull, the quarter slot
player is risking $375 per hour. That's already more than the $5
blackjack player, and there's more. The house edge is much
larger on slots than on blackjack. A typical quarter slot in Nevada
keeps about 6 percent of all the cash dropped into it; in Missouri
or Mississippi or other new gaming states, the house keeps about
8 to 10 percent. Even assuming the low 6 percent figure, that
makes the quarter slot player's expected average loss $22.50 per
hour—more than four times the expected loss for a $5 blackjack
player.

With that kind of expected loss, the quarter slot player can
expect to receive a buffet comp after a couple of hours instead of
having to play all day like a $5 blackjack player.

Of course, table players with a higher average bet size will
earn more and better comps more quickly. And even the $5 play-
ers are sometimes rewarded if they pick their spots. Binion's
Horseshoe in downtown Las Vegas is famous for being easy with
the breakfast comps for low-level bettors who play on the grave-
yard shift. But let the same player ask for a comp at the Mirage,
and the refusal will be mercifully quick.

10. True. Winning money will not disqualify you from receiving casino comps. The casino assumes you'll be back, and
eventually the house edge will catch up to you. Likewise, if you
have a larger than expected loss, your comp probably won't be
much bigger than if you'd just lost an average amount. The

casino assumes that over the long haul, you'll have wins as well as large losses, and they'll be comping you after both.

Instead of comping on the basis of individual wins or losses, they comp on mathematical expectation. The basic formula is Average Bet times Hands Played times House Edge equals Expected Loss. To plug in the numbers, for a $5 blackjack bettor, that comes to $5 average bet times 50 hands (for one house) times 0.02 for a 2 percent house edge equals $5 expected loss per hour. It doesn't matter if you've actually won $20 or lost $40, your comp is going to be based on that $5 expected loss.

Video Poker
Hand Number 1:
In the Beginning

What makes video poker tick? See if your general knowledge of this modern casino standard passes muster.

1. **Video poker was invented:**

   A. In the 1960s
   B. In the 1970s
   C. In the 1980s

2. **Among modern casino games, video poker's popularity ranks:**

   A. Second
   B. Third
   C. Fourth

3. **Most video poker is based on this live poker favorite:**

   A. Texas hold-'em
   B. Five-card stud
   C. Five-card draw

4. **Video poker differs from live poker in that:**

   A. The rank of hands is changed
   B. There are no opposing hands
   C. The odds of drawing good hands are lower

5. **Payoffs are determined by:**

A. Whether the player's hand beats a simulated dealer's hand
B. A pay table displayed on the machine
C. A jackpot button in the shift manager's office

6. **The video poker machine:**

    A. Deals from a randomly shuffled, fifty-two-card electronic deck
    B. Creates only ten cards at a time.
    C. Is programmed to deal you a specific percentage of winners.

7. **Video poker differs from slot machines in that:**

    A. We can tell the payback percentage by looking at the machine
    B. The deal is not random
    C. It costs more to play

8. **In basic Jacks or Better video poker, "8-5" and "9-6" refer to:**

    A. Odds against drawing a winning hand.
    B. Model numbers of two popular machines.
    C. Payoffs on full houses and flushes.

9. **When a player leaves a coin cup on top of a machine, it means:**

    A. "Cold machine—stay away."
    B. "Out of order."
    C. "I'll be back."

10. **In dealing the cards, the machine:**

    A. Deals a "shadow" hand behind your original five cards; any draws come from the cards "behind" your discards.
    B. Deals in sequence off the top of the deck.
    C. Continues to shuffle the remaining forty-seven cards until you set your discards.

11. The cards that you are dealt are determined:

A. By a random number generator.

B. By the number of hands you've played since your last winner.

C. By the number of coins you are playing.

12. The overall payback percentage:

A. Is unaffected by the number of coins you play.

B. Decreases as you pay more coins.

C. Is highest when you play maximum coins.

13. With expert play, the best video poker machines:

A. Pay back in excess of 97 percent of all coins played

B. Pay back in excess of 99 percent of all coins played

C. Pay back in excess of 100 percent of all coins played

14. The average video poker player:

A. Plays more than 2 percent shy of expert level

B. Plays more than 5 percent shy of expert level

C. Plays more than 10 percent shy of expert level.

15. In Bonus Poker and its variations—Double Bonus Poker, Bonus Poker Deluxe, Double Double Bonus Poker, Triple Bonus Poker—the "Bonus" refers to:

A. Extra payoffs on royal flushes.

B. Extra payoffs on fours of a kind.

C. Extra payoffs on pat winning hands with no draw.

16. Deuces Wild machines:

A. Pay their biggest jackpots on four deuces.

B. Pay their biggest jackpots on five of a kind.

C. Pay their biggest jackpots on royal flushes with no wild cards.

17. According to the State of Missouri, video poker:

A. Is a slot machine in disguise.

B. Is a game of skill.

C. Is not permitted.

18. A fast video poker player can play:

A. 800 or more hands per hour
B. 700 hands per hour.
C. 600 hands per hour.

19. The worst video poker games:

A. Are still worth playing.
B. Are better than most table games.
C. Are some of the worst games in the casino.

20. On the average, video poker paybacks:

A. Are lower than slot paybacks.
B. Are higher than slot paybacks.
C. Are about the same as slot paybacks.

Video Poker Hand Number 1: In the Beginning Answers

1. B. In the 1970s, versions of video poker were under development in the labs of both the Fortune Coin Company in Las Vegas and A-1 Supply in Reno. Si Redd, owner of Fortune, bought out A-1. From that merger grew IGT now the leading manufacturer of slot machines and other electronic gaming devices in the world. While under development in the '70s, video poker really made its breakthrough into casinos and start its rise to popularity in the early '80s.

2. B. Video poker is a close third, running neck and neck with blackjack as the second most popular game, behind slot machines. Both are far ahead of craps, which ranks fourth.

The more familiar the playing public gets with video poker, the more popular it becomes. If you've never visited a locals casino in Las Vegas, check it out sometime. At places like Palace Station, the Gold Coast and Orleans, there are fewer reel slot machines than you'll find on the Strip. Instead, you'll find row after row of video poker in seemingly countless varieties. Half or more the floor space in casinos that cater to Vegas locals is devoted to video poker. And that doesn't even take into account all the video poker bars in town. There's video poker in the grocery stores, laundromats and gas stations.

On the Strip, which attracts a tourist clientele, more like 17 percent of floor space is given to video poker. When new gaming jurisdictions started to open in the early 1990s, slot directors made the assumption that those tourist proportions would be right for their new casinos.

They were in for a shock. Video poker, it seems, is an acquired taste. The new riverboats and Native American casinos were attracting players who had never been to Las Vegas, Reno or Atlantic City, and those players weren't ready for video poker. They headed straight for the slot machines, where all they had to do was drop their money in and pull the handle. The slot director at Harrah's in Joliet, Illinois, told me he quickly had to reduce video poker's share of his floor from 17 percent to 10 percent.

Within a couple of years, that had started to turn. The more people play, the more they like the feeling of being at least a little in control, of actually affecting the outcome of play on a video poker machine. And the more they play, the more they discover that they get a better payback on even a mediocre video poker machine than on a reel slot. Slowly, newer casinos have been bringing the percentage of video poker machines back up. In riverboat states, with the space limitations that go with putting casinos on boats, video poker may never reach Nevada proportions, but demand will keep it high in the mix.

3. C. Almost all video poker is based on five-card draw, an interesting development because five-card draw is a rare game in casino poker rooms. Live poker tends to focus on stud games: seven-card stud, Texas hold-'em and Omaha hold-'em are the staples of casino poker.

Early in video poker's existence, there was an attempt to market a seven-card stud game. It flopped. Currently, there is a game based on Texas hold-'em and another based on five-card stud that hang on in the fringes of some casinos. The casino standards, the games that draw the players, are all based on five-card draw poker.

4. B. The bluffing and psychological aspects that make live poker such a thinking-person's game are gone from video poker. There is no one to bluff, no one to outfox. Whereas in live poker it's a must to know yourself and know your opponent as well as the cards, in video poker you simply must know the cards.

In live poker, any five-card hand can win, and almost any five-card hand can lose. How you play them is as important as what you're dealt. Not so in video poker. Here, the cards are everything. If you're dealt bad cards, the best-played bluff in the world can't make them win.

5. B. Video poker is played against a pay table that is either displayed on the machine's glass or on the video screen.

The basic pay table for the most common video poker game of the '80s, which is still played today, looks something like this:

DRAW POKER

Payoffs

	1 coin	2 coins	3 coins	4 coins	5 coins
Royal flush	250	500	750	1,000	4,000
Straight flush	50	100	150	200	250
Four of a kind	25	50	75	100	125
Full house	9	18.	27	36	45
Flush	6	12	18	24	30
Straight	4	8	12	16	20
Three of a kind	3	6	9	12	15
Two pair	2	4	6	8	10
Pair of Jacks or better	1	2	3	4	5

There are several notable things about this pay table, the "9-6" version of Jacks or Better draw poker. First, the ranking of poker hands is exactly the same as in live poker. It's easy. It's familiar. Anyone who has ever played poker around the kitchen table can grasp the concepts behind video poker in a heartbeat, and even those few Americans who have never played poker should be able to catch on fast.

Second, there is a large jump in the jackpot for a royal flush if you play the maximum number of coins allowed. Most video poker machines accept up to five coins at a time, though I've seen machines that take 10, and even 20 coins at a time. The higher number of coins taken usually are on nickel or penny machines. (Yes, there are penny video poker machines. Check out an area called "The Copper Mine" in the back of the Gold Spike casino in downtown Las Vegas.)

This pay table has stood the test of time enough so that not only is it still in use, it has been used as the basis for all others that have followed. All video poker machines use similar pay tables. All that changes is the amount paid for each hand. The pay table is varied to raise the house edge, to lower the house edge, to create bonuses that make the games more attractive to players and to balance off the bonuses. But the concept of player vs. pay table remains the heart of the game.

6. A. Cards are dealt from a randomly shuffled, fifty-two-card electronic deck. (In Joker's Wild, a fifty-three-card electronic deck is used.).

Just as with modern slot machines, video poker machines are really mini-computers. They have a microprocessor within. The program that determines what cards are dealt is called a "random number generator" or "RNG." The RNG runs continuously, even when no one is playing the machine. It generates numbers that correspond to possible hands, and when the player drops a coin into the slot, or hits the button to play one coin or maximum coins, cards are set for the coming hand.

Timing is everything as much in video poker as in anything else. It takes only microseconds for the RNG to generate a new number. If you stop to say hello to the cocktail waitress before pushing the button, you'll receive an entirely different hand than if you'd hit the button straight away. That means there's no need to fret if someone walks up to a machine you'd just left and hits a royal flush. Unless your timing was same down to the exact split second, you wouldn't have hit the royal.

All jurisdictions require the deal to be random, but just what they mean by random can differ radically from state to state. Nevada law requires that each card have the same chance to be dealt as any other. This makes video poker as random a game as human limitations in programming an RNG will allow. The effect is that you have the same game on a video poker screen as you'd get if a dealer were shuffling a physical deck of cards.

When Frank Scoblete was researching *Victory at Video Poker*, he found that some states had requirements in line with Nevada's, but some did not. Illinois, for example, requires a truly random card game, but New Jersey does not. New Jersey requires randomness in the same way it requires slot machines to be random: winning hands can be programmed to turn up with a specific frequency, but the specific times they turn up must be random.

In practice, it appears likely that all video poker machines made by major manufacturers conform to Nevada's tougher randomness standard. Nevada requires manufacturers in its state to abide by its standards, regardless of where the machines are being sold. And sources within the casino industry have told me they use the same computer chip in the same machine, regardless of location.

7. A. Because we know the cards are being dealt from a randomly shuffled fifty-two-card deck, we can calculate the frequency with which hands should occur. By applying that frequency of hands to the listed pay table, we can calculate a payback percentage for any video poker game.

Just by looking at the pay table in number 5, we know that with expert strategy in the long run it will return 99.5 percent of all coins played. There's plenty of room for short-term variation. Play $20 worth of quarters, five at a time, and it's possible to lose 16 hands in a row and wind up with nothing. It's also possible to hit a royal flush and win $1,000. But over hundreds of thousands of plays, the frequency of winning hands and the pay table say experts should get back 99.5 percent of everything they put in.

If the casino wants to change the payback percentage, it must change the pay table. I went on a Caribbean cruise a few years ago that had a number of Jacks or Better video poker machines on which full houses paid only 6-for-1 instead of the 9-for-1 in number 5, and flushes also were lowered from 6-for-1 to 5-for-1. Just by looking at it and reading the pay table, we know this is only a 95 percent machine and that our money's going to go a lot faster than on the 99.5 percent version.

We can't do this with reel slots. You can have two Red White and Blue machines sitting right next to each other, looking exactly alike. One is programmed for 99 percent payback, the other for 80 percent. Which is the good machine and which is the coin gulper? You pay your money and you take your choice. There's no way to tell from the outside.

8. C. Full house and flush payoffs are most common places payoffs are changed to alter the overall payback percentage.

A 9-6 machine pays 9-for-1 on full houses and 6-for-1 on flushes. An 8-5 machine pays 8-for-1 on full houses and 5-for-1 on flushes. That makes a big difference. Remember that 99.5 percent figure from number 5? That's what 9-6 Jacks or Better pays to experts in the long run. With an 8-5 pay table, Jacks or Better returns only 97.3 percent with expert play.

That's a difference worth your attention. Those who read the blackjack section of this book will know that the house advantage over a basic strategy player comes to about 0.5 percent. That's the equivalent of the house edge in 9-6 Jacks or Better—a 99.5 percent return yields a 0.5 percent house edge. Blackjack and good video poker games have similar house edges. However, just minor tinkering on full house and flush payoffs give 8-5 Jacks or Better a 2.7 percent house edge, soaring past the edges on good casino games like blackjack, and the best bets in craps and baccarat. In 6-5 Jacks or Better, like I found in the cruise ship in number 7, the house edge is 5 percent, right up there with roulette and Caribbean Stud.

For some reason, some players never learn to look at the numbers. The Tropicana in Las Vegas used to have a bank of quarter machines that alternated between 9-6 and 8-5 pay tables. My wife and I were aghast to see players seated indiscriminately, with as many at 8-5 machines as at 9-6ers. They were as much as telling the casino, "Here, take 2 percent of my money off the top."

The same principle applies with video poker games other than straight Jacks or Better. In Bonus Poker, you want to look for 8-5 pay tables, and in Double Bonus, you want 10-7 on the full house and flush. Each digit that one of these numbers is lowered drops your long-term expected payback by a little more than 1 percent.

Deuces Wild is a different animal. With four wild cards in the deck, probabilities are greatly altered. Changes can come all over the pay table. But if you look for machines that pay 5-for-1 on four of a kind, you won't go far astray. For more on Deuces, see number 16.

9. C. Video poker players abide by much of the same etiquette as slot players. A coin cup on the screen or on the seat means the machine is taken; the player has gone for a short break. If you're the player taking the break, though, don't make it too long. Depriving someone else of the chance to play while you disappear for a meal or for anything longer than a bathroom break or to find the change girl is needlessly selfish.

Even on short breaks, use common sense. Not long ago, I was standing behind a bank of nickel video poker machines at Boulder Station in Las Vegas when I saw a man get up to take a break. He had several hundred credits on the machine, but he just placed an empty coin cup on top of his screen to indicate the machine was occupied. All well and good, but while he was gone, a woman a few seats down decided to cash out. She had no coin cup, so she reached for the nearest one—the cup holding the first player's place. Easier than just asking someone to pass her a cup, I guess. When the man returned about 10 minutes later, no one had even approached his machine, so there was no harm done.

One little slot players' vice video poker players should lose is playing two machines at a time. With a reel slot, you can hit the button on one, then while the reels are spinning, push the button on another without losing any necessary concentration. I can almost understand players thinking that maybe by playing two machines, they'll catch one loose one with a high payback percentage. As long as the casino isn't crowded and there aren't people waiting for machines, it's not a problem.

Video poker is different. It requires decisions. A video poker player can't concentrate on necessary decisions and still keep up to speed on two machines. Most can't even play as many hands per hour on two machines as they could if they focused all their attention on one. Players who try two machines gain little, may even lose by making poor decisions, and keep someone else from playing.

10. B. This has changed in recent years. The original video poker machines were programmed to deal ten cards at a time, with five cards as a shadow hand behind the five you saw on the screen. If you discarded the card in position number 1, all the way to the left on the screen, it was replaced by the card "underneath" it in shadow position number 1.

That took away a lot of the reason for second-guessing. If a player had a Jack of clubs in position number 1 and King of spades in number 3, some early video poker books said to hold only the Jack. (Today we'd hold both the Jack and King.) If the player threw away the King of spades and a King of clubs popped up in its place, the player in the know could say, "I wouldn't have drawn that card if I'd kept the King anyway." On new machines, however, the cards are dealt in sequence. You see five cards on the screen. If you discard one card, regardless of position on the screen, you'll receive the next card off the top of the deck. There are still some older machines out there that deal the old way. It doesn't make any real difference, as long as the cards are random.

11. A. The random number generator determines which cards are dealt. It doesn't matter what cards have been dealt in previous hands. The odds of receiving any given hand are the same with each play.

Let's take four of a kind as an example. In Jacks or Better, four of a kind shows up about once per 425 hands. In something like Double Bonus Poker, in which we adjust our strategies to account for increased payoffs on four of a kind, we actually hit four of a kind a little more often.

Now, 425 hands per hour is a pretty easy pace for an average video poker player, so I usually tell readers that on the average, they should hit four of a kind about once per hour. There'll be hours with no quads, and hours with two or three, but in the long run, that's about how often they occur.

If you've just hit four of a kind, what are the chances of hitting quads again on the next hand? Still 1 in 425. Having just hit them in no way increases or decreases the odds against hitting again on the next hand.

Once I was playing quarter video poker on the Hollywood Casino City of Lights II in Aurora, Illinois. I hadn't intended to play at all that day; I was just making my periodic rounds to see what was new on the boat—whether blackjack rules had changed, new slot machines, changes in floor layout. I finished what I had planned and had about half an hour to the end of the cruise, so I pulled a $20 bill out of my wallet and went to play.

Within a few minutes, I hit four of a kind. I cashed out, and moved to the next machine. Another four of a kind. After a couple more hands, I cashed out again, and tried a third machine. FOUR more fours of a kind within ten minutes. I started to cash out—it was about time to go—but the hopper jammed and I had to wait for a slot technician. While waiting, I played the next machine and hit three more sets of quads. Half an hour of play, four of a kind nine times. It happens—just not very often.

12. C. The overall payback percentage is highest with maximum coins played, because playing the fifth coin makes you eligible for the bonus on royal flushes. Remember, a royal flush brings 1,000 coins with four played, but with five played the return jumps to 4,000.

Let's say you're playing 9-6 Jacks or Better, with an average long-term payback percentage of 99.5 percent. What is your expected return if you play only one coin at a time? Because the royal is worth less at this level, your average payback for one coin played is 98.1 percent. The same goes for two, three or four coins. But on that fifth coin, where the value of the royal rises, the payout percentage skyrockets. For the fifth coin only, the average long-term return is 105.6 percent, and that brings the overall average to 99.5 percent.

Does that mean you should always play maximum coins? Not necessarily. To start with, the player's bankroll is always the overriding consideration. Someone who brings $20 to the casino and expects a couple of hours of entertainment on quarter machines can't play five coins at a time. If there are no nickel machines available, the best solution is to play one coin at a time. It's not the best percentage play, but it'll enable the short-bankrolled player to get a longer run for his money.

Also, differences in pay tables may justify short-coin play. Let's say a player has sufficient bankroll to play five quarters at a time on an 8-5 Jacks or Better machine, paying 97.3 percent with expert play. But in the same casino he finds 9-6 Jacks or Better at the dollar level. He doesn't have the money to play maximum coins on dollars, but by playing one coin at a time on the dollar machine, he's actually getting a better payback percentage than he gets by playing maximum coins on quarters.

Of course, if our short-bankrolled player hits a royal flush, the naysayers will come out of the woodwork to tell him what a shame it is that he only played one coin, that he'd have hit the big jackpot if only he'd played the max. Don't let the naysayers stand in the way of your good time. A royal is blast to hit, even if your bankroll limits you to one-coin play.

13. C. Up until now, we've talked a lot about 9-6 Jacks or Better and its 99.5 percent payback. That was the original big hit, and casinos have been trying to wean players onto lower-paying machines ever since. Along the way, higher-paying machines have been created. The following all return in excess of 100 percent with expert play:

- 10-7 Double Bonus Poker (100.2 percent).
- 25-15-9-5-3 Deuces Wild (100.7 percent).
- 20-10-10-4-4 Double Pay Deuces (101 percent)
- 20-10-8-4-3 Triple Pay Deuces (100 percent)
- 25-17-10-4-3 Loose Deuces (101.6 percent)
- 20-7-5-3 Joker Poker (100.6 percent)

That is not an all-inclusive list. There are other rarely seen games such as "Gator Poker," also known as "All-American Poker," which pays 8-for-1 on flushes, full houses AND straights. Other games go into positive territory if the casino puts a progressive jackpot on royal flushes.

But the games listed here are the most common 100-percent or better machines around. Note that four of them are variations of Deuces Wild. The numbers before the Deuces games stand for payoffs on royal flushes with wild cards, five of a kind, straight flushes, four of a kind and full houses. In addition, on hands with four deuces, Deuces Wild pays 200-for-1, Double Pay Deuces pays 400-for-1, Triple Pay Deuces pays 600-for-1 and Loose Deuces pays 500 for 1.

Deuces Wild requires a more complex strategy than Jacks or Better, and most players don't get the payback expected for experts. Even so, 100-percent-plus Deuces games have declined throughout the '90s. Regular 25-15-9-5-3 Deuces Wild is still fairly easy to find on the quarter level in Las Vegas, but it's all but extinct on dollars. The Double, Triple and Loose Deuces machines almost all carry lower pay tables now. Any of these games are difficult to find outside Nevada in their full-pay versions.

Likewise, 20-7-5-3 Joker Poker was extremely popular in the early '80s, then nearly faded from sight. It's made a little comeback in the late '90s.

Possibly the most widely available 100 percent-plus machine is 10-7 Double Bonus Poker. There are no wild cards, but the strategy table is a mile long and there are some tricky quirks. We'll look at Double Bonus Poker strategy in *Video Poker Hand Number 5.*

14. A. I've seen specification sheets on video poker games that manufacturers give to casinos, and they tend to list payback percentages that are 2 to 3 percent lower than the ones games analysts calculate after the games are on the floor. How well the average player does is affected by the complexity of the machine. Jacks or Better is relatively easy, and the average player probably plays about 2 percent below optimum. I once saw one casino's monthly spreadsheet with actual earnings by Deuces Wild machines, and for that month, customers played more than 3 percent below optimum.

The best solution is to practice whatever game you're going to play. There are several good computer programs. In rating hands for this book, I *used Stanford Wong Video Poker*. Other good ones include Panamint's *VP Tutor* and Masque's *Video Poker Strategy Pro.*

It's also possible, though much slower, to practice by dealing video poker hands with deck of cards. If you're using cards instead of a computer, check yourself against strategy tables such as those in Frank Scoblete's *Victory at Video Poker* or Lenny Frome's *Winning Strategies for Video Poker.*

15. B. Bonus Poker and its variations all feature increased payoffs for fours of a kind. Video poker is delicately balanced enough that any increase in one part of the pay table has to bring a decrease elsewhere. In Bonus Poker, the increases in four-of-a-kind payoffs are small enough that they can be balanced by changing payoffs on full houses and flushes, just as in Jacks or Better. An 8-5 Bonus Poker machine returns 99.1 percent in the long run.

But by the time we get to Double Bonus Poker, where all four of a kind payoffs are at least doubled, and there are big increases on four Aces and four 2s, 3s or 4s, just changing full houses and flushes isn't enough. So full houses, flushes and straights are all increased instead—to 10-for-1, 7-for-1 and 5-for-1 in the full-pay version—and the big hit comes on two pair. In Double Bonus, two pair pays only 1-for-1 instead of 2-for-1 in Jacks or Better or Bonus Poker. Halving the payoff on such a common hand makes Double Bonus a much different game from other Jacks or Better variations. It's a beatable game in the long run, but if you don't hit your share of fours of a kind, it can drive you out of action fast.

16. C. The big jackpot on Deuces Wild remains on royal flushes with no wild cards, but as we saw in number 13, there are some nice secondary jackpots on four deuces. Because in Deuces

Wild we always hold any deuce, natural royals occur less frequently than in other games. In 9-6 Jacks or Better, royals occur about once per 40,000 hands; in 25-15-9-5-3 Deuces Wild, it's more like once per 45,000 hands.

17. B. When riverboat casinos were legalized in Missouri, legislators had neglected a provision in the state constitution that prohibited games of chance. Casinos opened as scheduled, but were permitted to open only with games of skill, including video poker, blackjack and craps. Among games analysts, eyebrows were raised over the inclusion of craps—it's all a crapshoot, after all. Perhaps dice-skidders, who skillfully slide dice the length of the layout without turning them, would be welcome. That's a skill that can get you thrown out of most casinos. Eventually an amendment was passed and reel slots and roulette wheels were permitted to join the games of skill.

18. A. I've been timed at more than 800 hands per hour in tournament play. I usually play about 100 hands per hour slower than that. One thing such speed means is that the effect of the house edge is multiplied greatly. Multiple-deck blackjack and 9-6 Jacks or Better have about the same house edge, 0.5 percent, assuming basic strategy on blackjack and expert play on video poker. But the video poker player can expect to lose more money. At 50 hands per hour, a $5 blackjack player risks only $250, and with basic strategy narrowing the house edge to 0.5 percent, he expects to lose an average of only $1.25. A video poker player risking $5 a hand—maximum-coin play on a $1 machine—at a steady pace of 500 hands per hour risks $2,500 and expects to lose an average of $12.50 per hour—10 times as much as the blackjack player.

All that can be mitigated by slot club returns. There are slot clubs that pay more than 0.5 percent in cash back. Risk $2,500 in an hour, have 0.5 percent rebated as slot club cash back and you're getting back the same $12.50 you expect to lose. Some clubs are more generous, and some less. But if you dip down a level and play the 8-5 Jacks or Better machines or worse, no slot club will pay the 2.7 percent or so of your play that it takes to bring you back to even.

19. C. There is a bit of "let the buyer beware" about video poker. Players in the know home in on the differences between 9-6 and 8-5 Jacks or Better, or 10-7 and 9-7 Double Bonus Poker. But 8-5 Jacks or Better, at 97.3 percent, still yields a better payoff than most slot machines, and 9-7 Double Bonus, and 99.1 percent, is a better bet than most casino games.

Sometimes, casinos put games on the floor that are much worse, and they may trap the unwary. I found one at Majestic Star Casino in Gary, Indiana, once that offered all kinds of pay table enhancements. Royal flushes paid 5,000 coins with five played instead of the usual 4,000-for-5. Straight flushes paid 200-for-1 instead of 50-for-1; fours of a kind were all 40-for-1, full houses 10-for-1, flushes 7-for-1 and straights 6-for-1. That all looked terrific. But the hammer hit on both three of a kind—paying 2-for-1 instead of 3-for-1—and two pair—paying only 1-for-1 instead of 2-for-1. Overall, that's only a 91.4 percent game for experts, and the average player could expect less than 90 percent. Ugh.

There are too many possible variations to warn you off every bad machine. Your best defense is to learn the GOOD ones. Then if run across a pay table you don't recognize and can't tell if it's good or bad just by looking, don't play it until you can learn more about it.

20 B. I've seen 9-6 Jacks or Better machines from Nevada to Mississippi to Illinois to New Jersey, but how many 99.5 percent reel slots have I seen? None.

In downtown Las Vegas, with the highest average slot payouts in the United States, quarter payouts average a shade over 95 percent, dollars a shade under 96 percent. Through most of the country, quarters average about 90 to 92 percent, dollars about 93 to 95 percent.

We know by looking at a video poker machine how much it should pay out. Those who take the time to learn the machines, and take the time to learn the strategies, should never find themselves playing a machine with less than a 97 percent payback. Video poker players should find better machines than reel slots wherever they play.

Video Poker
Hand Number 2:
True or False Questions

See if you can sort out the facts about video poker from the misconceptions:

1. **Video poker is pretty much the same throughout the United States.**

    True
    False

2. **Video poker pay tables reflect the relative frequency of paying hands.**

    True
    False

3. **It is possible to win at video poker in the long run.**

    True
    False

4. **There are people who make a living at video poker.**

    True
    False

5. **Video poker machines deal fewer winning hands to players who use slot club cards.**

    True
    False

6. **Progressive jackpots make a difference in a machine's pay-back percentage.**

   True
   False

7. **The casino can change the payback percentage by flipping a switch.**

   True
   False

8. **The most common pay table changes among machines of the same type come on full houses and flushes.**

   True
   False

9. **Players should always hold any paying hand.**

   True
   False

10. **Players must fill out a tax form on any one-hand win of $1,200 or more.**

    True
    False

11. **The odds of hitting a royal flush are about 40,000-1.**

    True
    False

12. **Once you've hit a royal, the odds of hitting another on the next hand are about 1,600,000,000-1.**

    True
    False

13. **If you are dealt five cards to a royal flush, the odds of drawing the fifth are only 1 in 47.**

    True
    False

14. **On some video poker machines, players must push buttons to discard cards instead of pushing buttons to hold cards.**

    True
    False

15. **It was a major surprise in the casino industry that video poker became a hit while video blackjack flopped.**

    True
    False

16. **Some video poker machines require more than five coins to qualify for the top jackpot.**

    True
    False

17. **Casinos sometimes change pay tables in unexpected places to fool the player.**

    True
    False

18. **Hand-held video poker games are a good way to practice.**

    True
    False

19. **Video poker players can practice by dealing regular cards.**

    True
    False

20. **In most video poker games that don't have wild cards, the most valuable cards in the deck are Aces.**

    True
    False

Video Poker Hand Number 2: True or False Answers

1. False. There are regional differences in video poker. Joker Poker is more popular in New Jersey than in most of the rest of the country. That dates back to the beginnings of video poker in Atlantic City. By the time 9-6 Jacks or Better was a hit in Nevada, casino operators knew what a low profit margin the game had. New Jersey operators wanted a bigger edge, and they added Jacks or Better in low-paying 6-5 and 7-5 versions. The first reasonable-paying video poker game in New Jersey was 16-8-5-4 Joker Poker (the numbers refer to payoffs on four of a kind, full house, flush and straight) with a top jackpot of 4,000 coins for five played on five of a kind. The payback of 97.2 percent wasn't great by Nevada standards, but it was high enough to make this the first big video poker hit in Atlantic City.

Through much of the rest of the country, Bonus Poker and, especially, Double Bonus Poker are the big hits. In 1995, I took a trip to Mississippi and found no Double Bonus, but lots of 9-6 Jacks or Better, which is rare in the Midwest. I'm told that has changed, that the Bonus Poker variations also are big in Mississippi today.

Nevada, of course, is where you'll find the biggest selection of video poker. Full-pay machines are getting harder to find, especially on the Strip, but check out downtown and the locals casinos. The good stuff is still there.

2. False. I have a couple of readers who have trouble with this. They keep sending me proposals to change pay tables and more accurately reflect the frequency of winning hands. I tell them the idea isn't to make a precise mathematical model of poker; it's to create a game that's fun and easy to play and that makes money for the casino while giving the player a decent chance to win.

It's been so ever since 9-6 Jacks or Better was invented. Given optimal play, we hit about the same number of full houses, flushes and straights. Full houses actually occur most frequently at once per 87 hands, followed by straights at once per 89 and flushes at once per 91. Still, to keep the game familiar, easy and fun, video poker pays more for full houses than flushes, and more for flushes than straights, just as full houses outrank flushes, which outrank straights when we gather around the kitchen table for a little seven-card stud.

Deuces Wild gives us a more extreme case. In the 25-15-9-5-3 full-pay version, fours of a kind occur about once per 16 hands, same frequency as straights and more frequently than full houses (once per 50 hands) or flushes (once per 60).

The best thing to do with these little ranking anomolies is to enjoy them—and learn strategies that account for their effects.

3. True, provided you choose machines wisely, know optimal strategies, play accurately and have a sufficient bankroll.

The player who hopes to beat video poker in the long run must know his machines. If you choose to play a 97 percent game like 6-5 Bonus Poker, optimal strategy, accurate play and enormous bankroll can't begin to make up for that 3 percent edge you're spotting the house.

Even on the right machine, playing video poker is often a waiting game. Full-pay Deuces Wild returns 100.7 percent in the long run, but most sessions will be losers unless they include either a royal flush, paying 4,000 coins for five played, or four deuces, at 1,000 coins for five played. The expert who hopes to turn a profit in the long run must be able to sustain the losing sessions between big wins.

The same goes for Double Bonus Poker, in its 10-7 incarnation another beatable game at 100.2 percent. But the player must hit his share of fours of a kind to keep going in this volatile game; otherwise there are plenty of losing sessions between royal flushes or big four-Ace winners.

Short-term losses are inevitable. Patience and a big bankroll are needed to turn those into long-term wins.

4. True. Early in 1998, I met up with Jean Scott, the Queen of Comps and a video poker pro, at the Orleans in Las Vegas. She asked, "Do you want to see a team at work?" and pointed over to a bank of progressives. Every seat was taken by player being paid to play. That team would monopolize the machines until one of them hit the royal flush.

Sometimes there are conditions in video poker that make it profitable not just for one player, but profitable enough that someone employs a team of accurate players. That usually happens with machines that have a progressive jackpot for a royal flush. A percentage of each coin played is added to the jackpot until someone eventually hits a royal.

When the jackpot gets high enough, even a weak machine can be worth playing. Take 8-5 Jacks or Better, normally a so-so bet at 97.3 percent payback. On a $1 machine, when the royal flush jackpot rises to $8,960 instead of the normal $4,000 for five coins played, the machine "goes positive." Its overall payback percentage is up to 100 percent. When it gets sufficiently above 100 percent that a team leader figures he can make up the cost of paying his team plus a profit provided a team member hits the royal, the team moves in.

What do team members get out of it? Minimum wage, perhaps a bonus for the one who hits the royal. And lots of comps—playing with a team involves lots of $1 and above play with someone else's money. The team leader might require slot club cash back to be turned over, but he's not in line for all the meal comps, free rooms and first class treatment that go with high-level play.

5. False. The magnetic reader for slot club cards is not linked to the random number generator. The RNG, which determines which cards you get, does not "know" whether you're using a slot club card.

I've had readers tell me they get worse cards if they use their slot club cards. If they do, they're just having a bit of bad luck. Even if the casinos could pull off such an effect, they wouldn't want to. Slot clubs are there to promote customer loyalty. It's not going to make the customer any more loyal to short him on the payback.

6. True. We got into this a little bit in number 4, on video poker pros, but every change in the video poker pay table affects the overall payback percentage. If full houses pay 9-for-1 instead of 8-for-1, that's a plus for the overall payback. It's also a plus if a royal flush returns 4,001 coins instead of 4,000 for five played.

In the case of 8-5 Jacks or Better, a fairly common progressive game, the break-even point is 8,960 coins. That doesn't have to be in dollars, as in number 4. If quarters are your game, divide 8,960 by four and look for $2,240 on the progressive meter. At that point, you're playing a 100 percent game.

Some Nevada casinos even put progressive jackpots on 9-6 Jacks or Better. There, the break-even point is only about 5,000 coins. And I've seen progressives on 10-7 Double Bonus Poker, already a 100.2 percent game.

As a rule, the 4,000-coin royal flush payback is about 2 percent of a machine's overall return. Excluding royals, Jacks or Better pays about 97.5 percent; with a normal 4,000-coin royal, it pays 99.5. Every 1,000 coins on the progressive meter adds about .5 percent to the overall payback, so it only takes 1,000 extra coins to move 9-6 Jacks or Better to 100 percent, while it takes nearly 5,000 extra to turn the 8-5 game positive.

It doesn't work out quite so neatly as the games get more complex, but it's not a bad rule of thumb: half a percent for each 1,000 coins above 4,000 on a royal flush progressive.

7. False. To change payback percentages on video poker, the casino must replace a computer chip and change the pay table. Flipping a switch won't do it.

8. True. Except for wild card machines, we almost always describe a game by its full house and flush payoffs. We compare 9-6 and 8-5 Jacks or Better, or 8-5 and 7-5 Bonus Poker, and we have 10-7, 9-7 and 9-6 Double Bonus Poker. That's where the pay table changes as the casino raises or lowers the payback percentage.

9. False. Late in 1997, I was playing Deuces Wild at the Fiesta in northwest Las Vegas. I was dealt three deuces, along with a 6 and 9 of hearts—a straight flush worth forty-five coins on the full-pay Deuces machine. I knew that if I held the Deuces alone, the worst I'd wind up with would be twenty coins for four of a kind, and I'd have a chance at something even better than a straight flush. So I discarded the 6 and 9, pushed the draw button and up popped the fourth 2—a 1,000-coin bonanza.

In Jacks or Better, we break up flushes or straights if we have four cards to a royal flush. We break up high pairs with four cards to any straight flush, even if it's not royal. And in Double Bonus Poker, we even break up full houses for the chance to draw to three Aces. We hold most paying hands, but sometimes it's more profitable to try for something better.

10. True. If you hit any jackpot of $1,200 or more on an electronic gaming device, the casino is required to have you sign a tax form before it can pay you.

11. True. That varies a bit from game-to-game, along with our drawing strategy. We should hit a royal about once per 40,000 hands in Jacks or Better or Bonus Poker, once per 45,000 in Deuces Wild, once per 48,000 in Double Bonus Poker or once per 42,000 in Joker Poker.

12. False. If you hit one royal flush, the odds of hitting one again on the next hand are the same (1 in 40,000) as before you hit the first one. Before you start playing, the odds of hitting two in row are 1 in 40,000 times 1 in 40,000, or 1 in 1.6 billion. After the first one hits, the odds of hitting the second one drop to the same as hitting one at any other time—1 in 40,000.

Multiple royals do happen. I haven't yet had anyone report to me that they've hit on consecutive hands, but several have reported more than one in a day. A reader once phoned to say she had won $1,000 for a royal flush at Double Bonus Poker. After tipping the change girl who helped with the payoff, the player moved to a progressive machine. And a couple of hours later, that change girl was startled to see a royal flush on the screen of a 25-cent progressive machine. "Oh, it's YOU!" she exclaimed. My reader had hit a second royal, this time worth a progressive jackpot of $1,070.

13. True. To continue my story from number 12, one of my readers had hit her second royal flush of the day. After she had been paid, she hit the "Maximum Bet"' button one more time. And as the change girl and slot supervisor watched in amazement, four parts of a royal flush turned up on the screen.

At this point, the odds of hitting a second royal in a row and third of the day aren't anything astronomical like 1 in 1.6 billion or 1 in 40,000. They're only 1 in 47. There are fifty-two cards in the electronic deck. Five have been seen, leaving forty-seven available for the one-card draw. The chances of drawing one card to a royal flush are 1 in 47, and it doesn't matter how many royals have been hit in the immediate past. Alas, in this case, it was not to be. The one-card draw brought no payoff.

14. True. Players had to be especially careful on early machines, when versions with "discard" buttons were nearly as common as those with "hold" buttons. Today, nearly all machines require you to press a button—or touch the card on the screen, in the case of new touch-screen models—in order to hold a card.

15. True. In the early days of video technology, nearly everyone expected video blackjack to be the hit among casino games. There are many more blackjack players than poker players in casinos, and it seemed a natural.

Some players didn't trust that they were getting a random game in video blackjack. Others just preferred to play at a live table. And many video blackjack machines paid only even money instead of 3-2 on blackjack, making it much tougher to win at the video game. Meanwhile, video poker, a much different game than live poker, took off and made history.

16. True. In the mid-1990s, I encountered 7-5 Bonus Poker machines in the Midwest that required you to play eight coins to qualify for the 4,000-coin jackpot on a royal flush. That lowers the payback percentage several tenths of a percent from the 98 percent on regular five-coin 7-5 Bonus Poker. Other machines require ten coins or twenty coins to qualify for the top jackpot. That's meant to induce players to bet more, to get a 25-cent player to bet $2.50 or $5 at a time.

It's better for the player if fewer coins are required. The Mirage and Treasure Island both addressed that in the late 1990s with machines that were proportional throughout their pay tables, awarding 800-for-1 on royal flushes even with only one coin played.

17. True. A couple of years ago, I walked into the refurbished Hollywood City of Lights I Casino, a beautiful boat in Aurora, Illinois, and was surprised to find 8-5 Bonus Poker for quarter players. Before refurbishing, the quarter Bonus Poker on the boat was split between 6-5 and 7-5 versions. I was thinking I'd have to write a column note praising the upgrade when I noticed that three of a kind paid only 2-for-1. Aaargghh! Hollywood was taking away far more with the reduction on three of a kind than it added by paying more on full houses. It turns out 8-5 Bonus Poker that pays only 2-for-1 on three of a kind is a 91.7 percent game to experts. And if they're really experts, they avoid this game.

18. False. Players can build speed and get comfortable with the game on hand-held machines, and that's about all. Most hand-held games don't include strategy tables, and the ones that do often are inaccurate. The best way to practice is on a computer program that will warn you when you make a mistake.

19. True, though not easily. I learned Jacks or Better strategy by dealing hands from a deck of cards while sitting with a strategy sheet in front of me I checked all my plays against the strategy sheet before moving on. That's a slow way to go about it. Computers are much better.

20. False. In most non-wild card games, the most valuable cards are Jacks. That's because a Jack can be paired with another Jack to form a paying hand, and because Jacks leave open more possible straights than do other high cards. Straights that include Jacks can range from Ace-high to Jack-high. Straights that include Aces can only be Ace-high or Ace low. Those with Kings can be Ace-high or King-high, and those with Queens can be Ace, King or Queen-high.

The result is that even in Double Bonus Poker, with a 160-for-1 payoff for four Aces, a player is better off starting a hand with a single Jack than with a single Ace. Holding a single Jack in 10-7 Double Bonus while tossing away unmatched cards of mixed suits with no straight possibilities bring an expected value of 2.29—in the long run you'll hit enough winners to bring returns of 2.29 coins per five played. Substitute an Ace, and the expected value drops to 2.18.

With two or more of a kind, that changes. Now straights don't factor into the picture, and you'd rather have two Aces to draw for that potential 800-coin jackpot than two Jacks with their 250-coin potential for four of a kind.

Video Poker Hand Number 3: The Games

Video poker isn't one game. It's dozens of games, each with its own strengths and weaknesses and each needing strategy adjustments. See how well you know the ins and outs of different kinds of video poker games:

JACKS OR BETTER

1. **A player at an 8-5 machine instead of 9-6 can expect to lose money:**
   A. Twice as fast.
   B. Three times as fast.
   C. Five times as fast.

2. **A nickel 9-6 machine returns:**
   A. About 5 percent less than a $1 9-6 machine.
   B. About 5 percent more than a $1 9-6 machine.
   C. The same percentage as a $1 9-6 machine.

3. **On a 9-6-4,700 machine, the "4,700" refers to:**
   A. An increased payout for a royal flush.
   B. The model number of IGT's second series video poker console.
   C. The average number of plays it takes for the house edge to hold up.

BONUS POKER

4. **On the highest-paying Bonus Poker versions, the paybacks on full houses and flushes are:**

   A. 6-5
   B. 7-5.
   C. 8-5.

5. **Most Bonus Poker versions increase four-of-a-kind payoffs from the usual 25-for-1 to 40-for-1 on four 2s, 3s and 4s and 80-for-1 on four Aces. A few, called Aces and Faces, make it 80-for-1 on Aces and 40-for-1 on Jacks, Queens and Kings, with of 2s, 3s and 4s lumped with other quads at 25-for-1. Compared with other Bonus Poker games, this:**

   A. Increases the payback percentage.
   B. Decreases the payback percentage.
   C. Makes no difference.

DOUBLE BONUS POKER

6. **Double Bonus Poker increases payoffs on:**

   A. Four Aces and four 2s, 3s and 4s, like Bonus Poker.
   B. All non-face cards.
   C. All fours of a kind.

7. **On the highest-paying Double Bonus Poker versions, the paybacks on full houses and flushes are:**

   A. 9-6
   B. 9-7.
   C. 10-7.

8. **To make up for other pay table increases, Double Bonus Poker:**

   A. Is programmed to deal fewer fours of a kind.

B. Lowers the usual 50-for-1 straight flush payoff to 10-for-1—6-for-1 for the flush plus 4-for-1 for the straight.

C. Lowers the payoff for two pair from 2-for-1 to 1-for-1.

DOUBLE DOUBLE BONUS POKER

9. Double Double Bonus Poker has a big payoff for:

A. Four Aces without a draw.

B. Four Aces with a 2, 3 or 4 as the fifth card.

C. Four Aces with King, Queen or Jack as the fifth card.

DEUCES WILD

10. In the full-pay version of Deuces Wild, four of a kind pays:

A. 25-for-1.

B. 10-for-1.

C. 5-for-1.

11. In Deuces Wild, fours of a kind occur:

A. About half as often as full houses.

B. About as often as full houses.

C. More than twice as often as full houses.

JOKER'S WILD

12. Atlantic City Joker Poker often differs from that in Las Vegas in that:

A. It's big jackpot is on five of a kind instead of a royal flush.

B. The Joker cannot be used as a card lower than a 7.

C. No hands pay only 1-for-1.

13. The highest paying version of Joker's Wild pays off on Kings or Better, has the big payoff on a royal flush and on four of a kind, full house and flush lists paybacks of:

A. 15-7-5.

B. 20-5-4

C. 20-7-5.

FLUSH ATTACK

14. Once a certain number of flushes have been hit, a Flush Attack is triggered and the next flush pays 25-for-1—as much as a four of a kind. The original program had to be adjusted because:

A. Players didn't understand the concept and avoided the machines.

B. The payoffs were too generous and the machines lost money.

C. Sharp players waited to play until others triggered the Flush Attack.

DOUBLE DOWN STUD

15. One of the few video poker games based on stud poker, Double Down Stud:

A. Is one of the highest-paying games.

B. Offers the player the chance to double his bet if he has a winner.

C. Is played with two decks instead of one.

FIVE DECK FRENZY

16. In Five-Deck Frenzy, the player receives one card from each of five different electronic decks. Any discard is replaced by a card from the same deck. That:

A. Makes possible a large progressive jackpot.

B. Dramatically increases the odds against the player.

C. Makes no difference in the odds of drawing any given hand.

MULTI-PAY POKER

17. This game plays just like regular video poker, except:

  A. Four of a kind payoffs are lower.

  B. Full house and flush payoffs are lower.

  C. The player can receive more than one payoff on the
     same hand.

PICK FIVE VIDEO POKER

**18. Pick Five dramatically changes the way video poker is dealt
in that:**

  A. The player may pick any five numbers from 1 through
     52; the corresponding cards are his hand.

  B. Cards are dealt two at a time, with the player selecting
     one to keep.

  C. The machine deals two hands at once; the player picks
     one hand to keep.

DOUBLE UP

**19. Some machines have a "Double Up" option that allows the
player to double his earnings after any winning hand. He
must select one of four face down cards to beat a dealer's
card, also dealt face down. The chances of winning a Double Up hand are:**

  A. 1 in 1.

  B. 1 in 2.

  C. 1 in 4.

**20. After having won three Double Up hands in a row, the
chances of winning a fourth are:**

  A. 1 in 2.

  B. 1 in 16.

  C. 1 in 64.

Video Poker Hand Number 3: The Games Answers

1. C. Let's say you're playing 25-cent 9-6 Jacks or Better video poker, five coins at a time at a nice, steady pace of 500 hands per hour. You're wagering $625 per hour. On the average, with expert play, you lose 0.5 percent of that, or $3.125. OK, you can't really lose the 12 ½ cents. Just figure your expected losses at an average of a little more than $3 per hour. That's not bad; in fact, it ranks with the best games in the casino. At that rate, you have a good shot to win. Hit four of a kind twice in an hour, or get a nice 250-coin payout for a straight flush, or even hit eight or nine full houses instead of your normal expectation of five or six and you probably walk away with a profit. You could also have one of those sessions when you go through six or eight $10 rolls of quarters without making any headway. Losses happen, but this at least is a game that gives you a shot.

Wagering at the same pace on an 8-5 machine, your expectation is to lose 2.7 percent of that $625. That's an average loss of nearly $17 per hour—$16.875, to be precise. That's a lot to overcome. Yes, it's possible to have a winning session, but the losses are going to be much more frequent. Look at it this way: with expected average losses of $3 per hour, you're spotting the machine a little more than the cost of two hands per hour. At nearly $17 per hour, you're spotting the machine a bit more than 13 hands per hour. It's almost like you've lost 13 hands before starting to play.

If the jurisdiction where I'm playing offers nothing better

than 8-5 Jacks or Better, I'll usually stick to table games. I don't even think about playing Jacks or Better if the pay table is 7-5 (96.2 percent, expected losses per hour of $23.75 per hour) or 6-5 (95 percent, losses of $31.25 per hour).

2. C. A 9-6 machine is a 9-6 machine, regardless of denomination. The same goes for any other video poker pay table.

Players have an image of nickel machines paying less than higher denominations. And it's true; casinos do try to squeeze a little more out of nickel play to make the machines profitable. Nickel slots usually are programmed to pay a lower percentage than quarter slots, which in turn pay less than dollar slots. But the way it's done on video poker is to change the pay table. You might look at a nickel machine and see that full houses pay only 6-for-1 and flushes pay 5-for-1. That's a 95 percent machine with expert play, and I wouldn't play it for quarters or dollars. But a nickel player might see it as a better option than playing slots of indeterminate payback. At least on the video poker machine, you know what to expect before you start.

3. A. Most widely available in downtown Las Vegas, 9-6-4,700 machines pay 4,700 coins for a royal flush hit with five coins played. That raises the overall payback percentage to 99.85 percent. It also squeezes under the IRS requirement for reporting jackpots. Casinos are required to report slot jackpots of $1,200 or more; at 4,700 quarters, the royal flush jackpot is $1,175.

4. C. In its full-pay 8-5 version, Bonus Poker pays 99.2 percent. At 7-5, that falls to 98.0 percent and at 6-5 it's 96.9 percent. The bonuses on fours of a kind (see question number 5) don't quite make up for the decrease in full house and flush payoffs.

Nevertheless, Bonus Poker has proved popular. It gave players a chance for a nice secondary jackpot on four Aces—$100 for quarter players—and started the trend that led to the even more popular Double Bonus Poker and other variations.

5. A. Aces and Faces, a proprietary game at Binion's Horseshoe in downtown Las Vegas, increases the payback percentage slightly, to 99.3 percent compared with 99.2 on regular 8-5 Bonus Poker. Having the bonuses come on fours of a kind with face cards helps. We keep a single King, Queen or Jack and occasionally luck into a four of a kind, whereas we'd just discard a single low card unless there was reason to keep it as part of a flush or straight.

6. C. All fours of a kind have big payoffs in Double Bonus. The garden variety quad—four 5s through Kings—pays 50-for-1 instead of the common 25-for-1 in Jacks or Better or Bonus Poker. Four 2s, 3s or 4s pay 80-for-1 and four Aces pay 160-for-1. Assuming five coins played, that means a 250-coin return for most quads, 400 coins on four 2s, 3s or 4s or 800 coins on four Aces.

Those are nice secondary jackpots. I remember one evening at the Stardust in Las Vegas, one of those nights when nothing was going right. I'd had three losing sessions at the blackjack tables, and had been piddling away quarters at video poker. It was fairly early, but I'd determined that the next $100 I played would be my last for the night, then it was time to eat and head to bed, or at least to catch up on some reading. I slid the $100 into a $1 Double Bonus machine, and on my fifth hand I hit four Aces. Boom! Eight hundred dollars. Then, 14 hands later, four 2s. Four hundred dollars. I was well again. My losses had been covered, and then some. Instead of slinking into Ralph's Diner for a hamburger, I sauntered into William B's steak house. THEN I called it a night, went to my room and did some reading. I'm no fool. There was no reason to give that money back.

Double Bonus can be invigorating when the quads come. When they don't . . . well, you wouldn't believe just how fast a $100 bill can go.

7. C. In addition to the four of a kind bonuses, Double Bonus Poker enhances paybacks on full houses, flushes and straights. On almost all versions, straights pay 5-for-1 instead of the 4-for-1 standard on Jacks or Better or Bonus Poker. That leaves full houses and flushes. At 10-7, Double Bonus returns 100.2 percent in the long run, making it one of the best-paying video poker machines. At 9-7, it pays 99.1 percent, and at 9-6 it pays 97.8 percent.

Those are the most common versions of Double Bonus. There is a variation on 9-6 Double Bonus that sometimes appears on Bally's Game Maker multiple-game machines. It pays 1,000 coins for five played on four Aces instead of the usual 800. That raises the 9-6 payback to 99.0 percent.

If you see a version of Double Bonus that does not pay at least 9-for-1 on full houses, 6-for-1 on flushes and 5-for-1 on straights, do not play it. I recently spotted an 8-5-4 version. That's down under 94 percent payback with expert play—and expert play on Double Bonus can be tricky.

8. C. The payoff on two pair is lowered to 1-for-1. That makes Double Bonus an extremely volatile game.

A reader told me all about her exploits at video poker—specifically, two sessions at Double Bonus Poker with wildly different results. She had made two visits to the same casino and played at the same bank of 25-cent 10-7 machines, with a progressive jackpot on the royal flush. On her first visit, the reader couldn't lose. She hit one of the garden variety four-of-a-kinds early, and since she was playing the full five coins, that gave her 250 quarters to play with. A little later she hit another. Four 3s was worth a bonus, another 400 coins. Then another four 3s.

There were just about twenty minutes left in the cruise, and she turned to a man next to her and said, "Now I'm going for the four Aces."

"Think big," he replied. "Go for the royal."

And that's what she did. Royal flush, worth more than $1,100.

Fast forward two weeks. Same player, same casino, same bank of Double Bonus Poker machines. Only this time she dumped roll after roll of quarters into the machine with very little return until she finally moved on. "I couldn't even get a little something to keep me going," she said, grimacing. "It was awful. How could it be so good one time and so bad the next?"

The short answer is that Double Bonus Poker can go from incredibly good to impossibly bad because it was designed that way. Just as in Jacks or Better, about 1 in 8 hands yields two pair. Two pair hands are so common that with a 2-for-1 payoff, they account for about one-quarter of all paybacks in Jacks or Better. In Double Bonus, that payback is halved, and replaced by increases on less common hands. That means you either hit the less common hands, and win big, or you don't, and you lose fast. Double Bonus is a streaky, uneven game with big wins and fast losses.

9. B. Double Double Bonus offers a 400-for-1 jackpot if the player draws four Aces with a 2, 3 or 4 on the fifth card. That's a 2,000-coin return for five played. It also pays 160-for-1—or 800-for-5—on four 2s, 3s or 4s with an Ace, 2, 3 or 4 as the fifth card. Other than that, the game looks a lot like Double Bonus. Four 5s through Kings pay 50-for-1, four 2s, 3s or 4s pay 80-for-1 and four Aces pay 160-for-1 if the fifth card doesn't trigger the bonus. The full-pay version, returning 98.8 percent, pays 9-for-1 on full houses and 6-for-1 on flushes. The payoff on straights drops back to 4-for-1 from the 5-for-1 on Double Bonus.

One strategy hint: if you have three Aces, 2s, 3s or 4s, plus a bonus card among the others off the deal, just hold the three of a kind. Do not hold a bonus card kicker. You dramatically reduce the chances of drawing four of a kind at all by giving yourself only one chance instead of two. You'll cost yourself money in the long run if you get greedy and play with a "bonus or nothing" attitude.

10. C. In full-pay Deuces Wild, four of a kind pays 5-for-1. Most Deuces Wild machines reduce four of a kind to 4-for-1. When I'm asked by a player who's going to be in an area that has full-pay Deuces what to look for, I point out the 5-for-1 on quads. There are other pay table variations, but that's the most important.

11. C. In all Deuces Wild versions, fours of a kind pop up more than twice as often as full houses. And in many versions, given optimal strategy, there are more than three times as many quads as full houses. In full-pay Deuces, for example, we hit four of a kind about once per 16 hands, while we hit a full house about once per 50 hands.

There are a couple of reasons for this. For one thing, we hold all deuces, and any two-pair hand that includes two 2s becomes four of a kind. A single deuce combined with a three of a kind also becomes four of a kind. Three deuces? Your hand is no worse than four of a kind.

There is no effect of that magnitude to increase full houses. A single deuce combined with two pair will produce a full house. Other than that, it's natural full houses all the way. It's impossible to wind up with a full house if you have more than one deuce. You'll jump straight from three of a kind to four of a kind if you pair up any other cards to go with two 2s.

Not only that, our playing strategy often limits our chances for full houses. When full houses pay only 3-for-1, as in full-pay Deuces Wild and most other Deuces games, we break up two-pair hands. Three of a kind is the minimum winner in most Deuces variations. So if we hold two pair, we either hit a full house or we lose. Hold only one pair, and we have a chance at three of a kind, full house, four of a kind or five of a kind. None of that's impossible with four wild cards in the deck.

There is an exception. One of the most common variations on Deuces Wild reduces the four-of-a-kind payoff to 4-for-1, but increases full houses to an equal 4-for-1 and flushes to 3-for-1. Insiders call this game "Illinois Deuces" because it rose to popularity at the Par-A-Dice casino in East Peoria, Illinois. It doesn't say Illinois Deuces on the machine glass, though, just Deuces Wild.

Anyway, in Illinois Deuces, we hold both pairs because of the increased full house payoff and the decreased four of a kind payoff. Still, four of a kinds pop up once per 16 hands, while full houses occur only once per 38 hands.

Some players think Illinois Deuces is a pretty good deal. Compare these pay tables:

	Full-pay Deuces	**Illinois Deuces**
Royal flush, no wild cards	800-for-1	800-for-1
Four deuces	200-for-1	200-for-1
Royal flush with wild cards	25-for-1	25-for-1
Five of a kind.	15-for-1	15-for-1
Straight flush	9-for-1	9-for-1
Four of a kind	5-for-1	4-for-1
Full house	3-for-1	4-for-1
Flush	2-for-1	3-for-1
Straight	2-for-1	2-for-1
Three of a kind	1-for-1	1-for-1

Some look at those tables and say, "Wow! I give up one unit on four of a kind, but I pick up one on full houses AND another on flushes. That's my machine!"

Uh-uh. In Deuces Wild, increases on full houses and flushes don't begin to make up for decreases in four of a kind payoffs. Flushes occur only once per 48 hands in Illinois Deuces. Even with strategy adjustments, in the time it takes to hit three fours of a kind, you'll average only one flush and one-and-a-fraction full houses. The overall payback percentage on Illinois Deuces is only 98.9 percent, compared with 100.7 on full-pay Deuces.

12. A. The breakthrough Joker's Wild game in Atlantic City paid 4,000 coins with five played on five of a kind. And while it's possible to find Joker Poker in New Jersey with the big jackpot on the royal flush, the local preference is for big bucks on five of a kind.

To an outsider, the pay table looks out of kilter in classic Atlantic City 16-8-5-4 Joker's Wild. The big jackpot comes frequently—once per 11,000 hands. Meanwhile, the natural royal flush at 100-1 pays no more than any other straight flush, with or without the wild card. That's true even though natural royals turn up only once per 63,000 hands.

The frequency of big jackpots—certainly a reason for the game's popularity—means the rest of the pay table has to be held down. The lowest paying hand is two pair on this 97.2 percent game. Compare that with full-pay Las Vegas Joker Poker, which puts the big payoff on the natural royal. Paybacks start at a pair of Kings or better, and with a 20-7-5-3 pay table on four of a kind, full house, flush and straight, the machine pays 100.6 percent with expert play.

13. C. Those 20-7-5 machines seemed all but extinct a few years ago, but seem to be making a comeback in some Las Vegas locals casinos.

14. C. There are a couple of different versions of Flush Attack. Sometimes several machines are linked electronically. Sometimes the program is specific to one machine. Either way, when a certain number of flushes are hit, the words "FLUSH AT-TACK" flash on the screen. During a flush attack, the next flush pays 25-for-1 instead of 5-for-1. Hitting a flush takes the machine out of attack mode until the next string of flushes activates it again.

Flush Attack originally linked banks of several machines. When the Flush Attack mode was on, it was on for all machines. Video poker pros caught on quickly that they could play until they were dealt a natural flush or four to a flush, then leave it on their screen until someone else triggered Attack mode. When FLUSH ATTACK flashed, then the pro would play out his hand and siphon off the bonus. Knowledgeable players got to skim off profits while tourists took all the risk.

The program was changed so that a new hand had to be started to be eligible for the Attack payoff. That helped, but didn't totally eliminate the waiting strategy. When tourists keep a bank of linked Flush Attacks busy, pros sit at a machine and wait to play until Attack mode is signalled.

15. B. Double Down Stud was introduced in the early '90s as a table game, but it was quickly decided that it works better as a video poker game. The player makes a bet, and four cards are dealt. Before receiving the fifth card, the player has the option of doubling his bet.

Winning bets are paid as follows: 1-for-1 on a pair of 6s through 10s; 2-for-1 on a pair of Jacks through Aces; 3-for-1 on two pair; 4-for-1 on three of a kind; 6-for-1 on a straight; 9-for-1 on flush; 12-for-1 on a full house; 50-for-1 on four of a kind; 200-for-1 on a straight flush, and 1,000-for-1 on a royal flush. The royal pays 2,000-for-1 if the initial bet is 10 coins or more.

Strategy is easy. Double your bet before your fifth card if you have a hand that already is a winner. Also double if you have four cards to a flush or four to an open-ended straight. That yields a long-term payback percentage of 97.8 percent.

16. A. Five Deck Frenzy has a progressive jackpot on five Aces of spades. Througout its pay table, it gives bonuses for "suited" hands—four of a kind of the same suit, three of a kind of the same suit. Full houses are considered suited even if the pair is in diamonds, for example, while the three of a kind is in spades.

Five Deck Frenzy gave video poker its first progressive jackpot large enough to rival some of the monster slot payments. The game has an overall payback of 98.8 percent for players who learn expert strategy.

17. C. On the face, Multi-Pay Poker looks like 8-5 Kings or Better, not Jacks or Better. There are some other pay table reductions—four of a kind, for example, pays only 20-for-1 instead of 25-for-1.

What makes it attractive is that the player is paid for each winning combination in the hand. Hit three Jacks and two Aces and you're not just paid for the full house, you're also paid for three of a kind, two pair and a high pair. That brings the payback up past 99 percent. Look for this game on Williams' Multi-Pay Plus multiple-game machines.

18. B. Pick Five made its way into Nevada in late 1997. It's essentially 9-6 Double Bonus with a big difference. Two cards are displayed; the player keeps one and discards one; two more are displayed, and the player again keeps one. There are five rounds of this until the player has his final five-card hand. With the following pay table, the developers say payback calculates to 103 percent with computer perfect play: royal flush, 800-for-1; straight flush, 50-for-1; four Aces, 160-for-1, four 2s, 3s or 4s, 80-for-1; four 5s through Kings, 40-for-1; full house, 9-for-1; flush, 6-for-1; straight, 4-for-1; three of a kind, 3-for-1; two pair, 1-for-1; pair of Jacks or better, 1-for-1.

The developers think players will play enough below optimal that the casinos will make money on the game. A computer can keep track of discards and calculate their effect on the percentages of later draws, and most people won't be able to do that.

19. B. Double Up is an even bet. There is no house edge. You are just as likely to have the higher card as the dealer. Slot clubs give no points for your Double Up wagers.

So should you play Double Up? That depends. Do you like to? I got a letter once from a fellow who played in a casino that offered only mediocre pay tables on video poker. However, the machines all carried the Double Up option. My reader found he did better on Double Up than on the regular game, and had settled into always doubling on 1-for-1 and 2-for-1 payoffs.

Myself, I like playing video poker. Given a decent machine, I'll stick to video poker and skip the Double Up every time.

20. A. No matter how many times you've won in a row, the chances of winning the next one are 1 in 2. It's the casino equivalent of flipping a coin. The same fellow who wrote to say he always doubled small payouts also said he'd usually try to double three times, but he wouldn't go to four because he'd heard there was only a 1 in 16 chance of successfully doubling four times in a row.

That's true before you start. The chances of doubling up four times in a row are 1 in 16. But once you've successfully doubled three times, you're no longer trying to double four times. You're just trying to double once, and the odds are 1 in 2. If you were to win that bet, the odds of winning the next, your fifth in a row, would again be 1 in 2. Each trial is an independent event, and past outcomes have no influence on independent events.

Video Poker Hand Number 4: Jacks or Better

The next four quizzes are going to deal with playing strategies. I've selected full-pay versions of four common varieties of video poker: 9-6 Jacks or Better, 10-7 Double Bonus Poker, 20-7-5 Joker Poker and 25-15-9-5 Deuces Wild. These are machines to look for. You won't always be able to find them, but if you start by learning the expert strategies for the full-pay versions, you won't be far off optimal play when you can find only lesser pay tables.

Jacks or Better, with no special bonuses and no wild cards, is the basic video poker game. Master this game, and you have a big head start on learning to play others. In fact, Jacks or Better strategy can be applied directly to Bonus Poker with no appreciable loss in accuracy. And expert strategy that yields a 99.5 percent return in 9-6 Jacks or Better works even better in 10-7 Double Bonus Poker, yielding 99.8 percent (expert strategy specific to 10-7 Double Bonus yields 100.2 percent).

Answers here are based on the 9-6 version of Jacks or Better. Assuming five coins played, the pay table starts at 800-for-1 on a royal flush, with 50-for-1 on a straight flush, 25-for-1 on four of a kind, 9-for-1 on a full house, 6-for-1 on a flush, 4-for-1 on a straight, 3-for-1 on three of a kind, 2-for-1 on two pair and 1-for-1 on a pair of Jacks or Better. We assume five coins played because playing max coins leaves open the big bonus on a royal flush. If you play fewer than five coins, royals pay only 250-for-1.

Mastering 9-6 Jacks or Better is more than half the battle in video poker. Test your knowledge on the hands below:

1. **You're dealt King of clubs, 9 of spades, 7 of hearts, 4 of diamonds, 4 of clubs:**

   A. Hold the King.
   B. Hold the pair of 4s.

2. **You're dealt King of clubs, 9 of spades, 8 of hearts, 7 of diamonds, 6 of clubs:**

   A. Hold the King.
   B. Hold the four-card straight.

3. **You're dealt King of clubs and 8-6-4-3 of hearts:**

   A. Hold the King.
   B. Hold the four-card flush.

4. **You're dealt 9 of spades, 8 of hearts, 7 of clubs, 6 of clubs and 6 of spades:**

   A. Hold the four-card straight.
   B. Hold the pair of 6s.

5. **You're dealt 8-6-4-3 of hearts and 6 of spades:**

   A. Hold the four-card flush.
   B. Hold the pair of 6s.

6. **You're dealt Queen of spades, Jack of hearts, 7 of spades, 5 of hearts, 2 of clubs:**

   A. Hold the Queen.
   B. Hold the Jack.
   C. Hold Queen and Jack.

7. **You're dealt Ace of diamonds, Queen of spades, Jack of hearts, 5 of hearts, 2 of clubs:**

   A. Hold the Ace.
   B. Hold the Queen.
   C. Hold the Jack.
   D. Hold Queen-Jack.
   E. Hold Ace-Queen-Jack.

8. **You're dealt King of diamonds, Queen of spades, Jack of hearts, 5 of hearts, 2 of clubs:**

    A. Hold the King.
    B. Hold the Queen.
    C. Hold the Jack.
    D. Hold Queen-Jack.
    E. Hold King-Queen-Jack.

9. **You're dealt King of spades, Queen of spades, Jack of hearts, 5 of hearts, 2 of clubs:**

    A. Hold King-Queen.
    B. Hold King-Queen-Jack.

10. **You're dealt Ace of spades, King of hearts, Jack of clubs, 10 of spades, 4 of clubs:**

    A. Hold Ace-King-Jack-10.
    B. Hold Ace-King-Jack.
    C. Hold King-Jack.

11. **You're dealt King of hearts, Jack of clubs, 10 of spades, 9 of diamonds, 4 of clubs:**

    A. Hold King-Jack-10-9.
    B. Hold King-Jack.
    C. Hold the King.
    D. Hold the Jack.

12. **You're dealt King-10-8 of diamonds, 6 of clubs, 2 of spades:**

    A. Hold all three diamonds.
    B. Hold King-10.
    C. Hold the King.

13. **You're dealt 9-8-7 of diamonds, 7 of spades, 3 of hearts:**

    A. Hold the three-card straight flush.
    B. Hold the low pair.

14. **You're dealt King-Queen-Jack-10 of diamonds and Queen of clubs:**

   A. Hold the four diamonds.
   B. Hold the pair of Queens.

15. **You're dealt King-Queen-Jack-10 of diamonds and Ace of spades:**

   A. Hold the four diamonds.
   B. Hold the straight.

16. **You're dealt 6-7-8-9 of clubs and a 10 of hearts:**

   A. Hold the four-card straight flush.
   B. Hold the straight.

17. **You're dealt 6-7-8-9 of clubs and a 9 of hearts:**

   A. Hold the four-card straight flush.
   B. Hold the pair of 9s.

18. **You're dealt King of spades, Queen of diamonds, Jack of hearts, 8 of hearts, 7 of hearts.**

   A. Hold King-Queen-Jack.
   B. Hold Queen-Jack.
   C. Hold the Jack.
   D. Hold Jack-8-7.

19. **You're dealt 6-9-10 of hearts, 2 of spades and 4 of clubs.**

   A. Hold the three hearts.
   B. Discard all five cards.

20. **You're dealt 5-9-10 of hearts, 2 of spades and 4 of clubs.**

   A. Hold the three hearts.
   B. Discard all five cards.

Video Poker Hand Number 4: Jacks or Better Strategy Answers

1. B. One of the first things new video poker players need to learn is that holding a single high card is a relatively weak start to a hand, and that a low pair is actually a pretty good start. Start with a low pair, match one card on the draw and you have three of a kind. A low pair is a good start toward two pair, even full houses and four of a kind.

To rate pre-draw hands, video poker analysts calculate an "expected value" or "EV." The expected value is an average of all the things the pre-draw hand could become if all the possible draws are taken into account. In this case, the pair of 4s has an expected value of 4.12. Assuming you're playing five coins at a time, your average expected return if you hold the pair and discard the other cards is 4.12 coins. Often you'll get nothing, but there'll be enough winners in there that you'll get back about 80 percent of your bets in the long run.

The EV for holding only the King in this hand is 2.37. It may seem like you have a better chance to draw a winner by holding the King and taking four shots at pairing it up, but that's just what the majority of your winners will be—a high pair returning five coins. You'll take in more money in the long run by holding the low pair.

2. B. That four-card straight isn't as strong a starting point as a low pair, but it's still better than a lone King. Even though the four-card straight can't develop into any winners other than a straight, you'll complete it often enough that its EV of 3.40 out-strips the 2.35 for the King.

Incidentally, notice that the EV for the King is a tiny bit lower in number 2 than in number 1. That happens every time we change the cards in the initial deal, and it's nothing to be concerned about. The computer program I use takes into account the effect of discards on the remaining draw possibilities, resulting in small fluctuations in values.

3. B. Flushes are more valuable than straights, and we're able to complete four-card flushes a bit more often than we complete four-card straights. So if the four-card straight is more valuable than the King in number 2, the four-card flush is more valuable than the King here. Right?

There are thirteen cards in each suit, so when we start with four cards to a flush, there are nine cards among the remaining forty-seven that will make our hand. With a four-card open-ended straight, as in number 2, we have eight chances to make our hand. With 6-7-8-9 of mixed suits, we complete a straight with any of the four 5s in the deck or any of the four 10s. The flush also pays 6-for-1 in 9-6 Jacks or Better, and 5-for-1 in other pay tables, compared with 4-for-1 for the straight.

With a four-flush vs. a single high card, it's not close. The four-flush has an expected value of 5.74. With this start, in the long run, we'll actually get back more than we put into the machine. The lone King hangs in there at 2.39.

4. B. A bunch of you probably picked up on numbers 1 and 2 and decided, "Aha! The low pair, with more possibilities, stronger than the four-card straight." Yep. For those who like numbers, the EV is 4.12 on the pair, 3.40 on the four-card straight.

5. A. The four-card flush is the one hand we've discussed so far that brings us more money than we bet in the long run. Keep the hearts (EV 5.74 on the four-flush, 4.12 on the low pair).

6. C. Two high cards is a stronger starting point than one high card. With two high cards at the start, you have a better chance of pairing one of them for paying hand, and there are possibilities for two pair, three of a kind, full houses, four of a kind, even straights.

Starting with two high cards is not a strong as some of the other hands we've looked at. The EV of Queen-Jack here still is only 2.55, but that's about 10 percent higher than the EVs in the 2.30 neighborhood we get for single high cards.

Interestingly, early video poker texts recommended holding only the lowest high card in the hand. The reasoning was that drawing more cards would give you a better chance to pair up the one card you held, and by holding the lowest high card you were giving yourself the most straight possibilities. The more detailed computer analyses of the game that followed showed that the player actually has a better chance to win by holding both high cards.

7. D. Aces get in the way of straights. When you hold an Ace with other high cards, the only possible straights are Ace high.

The advantages of holding two high cards outweigh the limitations on straights, so if your options were Ace, Jack and three low cards of mixed suits, you'd hold both the Ace and the Jack. Here, though, the better play is just to hold two high cards while discarding the Ace. The EV of holding Queen-Jack here is 2.50. The EVs of the other four options given all are under 2.30.

8. E. Three unpaired high cards with King high leave open both King-high and Ace-high straights. That's enough of a difference from number 7 that we hold all three high cards here. The EV of holding King-Queen-Jack is 2.57, to 2.48 of King-Queen. The others are less than 2.30.

9. A. We always have to have an eye on the big jackpot for a royal flush. Better to keep two high cards of the same suit than three of mixed suits. The EV for holding King-Queen of spades is 2.96; for King-Queen-Jack it's 2.57.

10. A. Poker players seem to learn in the cradle that they should never draw to inside straights. Ace-King-Jack-10 is an inside straight draw; the only cards that can complete the hand are the four Queens. That differs from an open-ended straight, which leaves eight possible finishing cards. If we had King-Queen-Jack-10 instead, any of the four Aces or any of the four 9s would give us a straight.

Nevertheless, in Jacks or Better video poker we do draw to inside straights if they include at least three high cards. In number 10, drawing any of the four Queens would give us our straight, but drawing any of the three remaining Aces, three Kings or three Jacks also would give us a winning hand. That's enough to make this the best option here, with an EV of 2.66 to 2.38 for King-Jack and 2.21 for Ace-King-Jack.

11. B. Another inside straight, but this time we have only two high cards. That tips the balance away from going for the straight. The best option here his holding King-Jack, with a 2.42 EV compared with 2.34 on King-Jack-10-9.

12. B. This is the closest call of any answer in this section. We do not hold three-card flushes in Jacks or Better, so the real question here is whether to hold King-10 or just the King. Holding a 10 isn't the same as holding another high card; it gives us no additional potential winning pairs of Jacks or better. All it does is to add potential for a flush, straight flush or royal flush. With an eye on the big royal payout, the decision by an eyelash is in favor of King-10. That has an EV of 2.31, compared with 2.30 for just the King.

13. B. We do hold three-card straight flushes, and with an EV of 3.09, the 7-8-9 of diamonds is not a bad pre-draw hand. But the pair of 7s, at 4.12, is quite a bit better.

14. A. Four-card royal flushes are powerful hands. We have a 1 in 47 shot at hitting the royal and that big 4,000-coin jackpot. In this case, we also could hit a straight flush with the 9 of diamonds. We have possible flushes with any of the seven other diamonds, straights with the other three 9s or other three Aces, and high pairs with the other three Jacks, Kings or other two Queens. Of the forty-seven possible draws, twenty-three are winners, and one is a huge winner.

It's no contest. We break up a winning hand. Holding the four-card royal has an EV of 98.30 compared with 7.68 for holding the pair of Queens.

15. A. Again, no contest. We break up the straight, giving away a sure 20-coin winner for the possibility of much more. The EV is 98.00 for the four-card royal, and we win a flat 20 coins by keeping the straight.

16. B. A four-card straight flush is nowhere near as strong as a four-card royal. Here, the EV of the four clubs is 17.23. It's not worth breaking up a 20-coin winner to take a 1 in 47 shot at a 250-coin payout.

17. A. The four-card straight flush is a much stronger hand than a low pair, however. Take your shot here, with a 17.66 EV on the four-card straight flush compared with 4.12 on the low pair.

18. D. We don't hold three-card flushes in Jacks or Better, but we do hold three-card straight flushes, even with two inside draws as in this example. Here, if we fill in a 9 and 10 of hearts between the 7-8 and Jack, we have a straight flush. It's a better bet than just holding high cards, with a 2.69 EV to 2.57 for King-Queen-Jack, the next best option.

19. A. This is another double-inside straight flush. Fill in a 7 and 8 of hearts between the 6 and the 9-10, and you have a straight flush worth 250 coins. The double-inside straight flush with no high cards is the lowest ranking hand worth holding. Here, holding 6-9-10 of hearts has an EV of 2.22 compared with 1.80 for chucking the whole hand.

20. B. With 5-9-10, there are no straight flush possibilities. Ignore the three card flush, and just start over. Discarding all five cards has an EV of 1.80, better than the 1.73 for the three-card flush.

Video Poker
Hand Number 5:
Double Bonus Poker

Double Bonus Poker has its roots in Jacks or Better, and you won't be too badly served by playing Jacks or Better strategy. That'll get you to 99.8 percent payback in the 10-7 Double Bonus game. But to get to expert level and squeeze out the last few tenths of a percent for the potential 100.2 percent payback is tricky.

Answers here are based on the 10-7 version of Double Bonus Poker. Versions with 9-7 and 9-6 pay tables also are common. Each has its own little strategy quirks—strategy quizzes on video poker variations could fill several answer books by themselves.

Assuming five coins played, the pay table for 10-7 Double Bonus starts at 800-for-1 on a royal flush, with 50-for-1 on a straight flush, 160-for-1 on four Aces, 80-for-1 on four 2s, 3s or 4s, 50-for-1 on four 5s through Kings, 10-for-1 on a full house, 7-for-1 on a flush, 5-for-1 on a straight, 3-for-1 on three of a kind, 1-for-1 on two pair and 1-for-1 on a pair of Jacks or Better.

See if you can make your way through the Double Bonus maze:

1. **Jack of hearts, Jack of clubs, 2 of diamonds, 2 of spades, 8 of clubs:**

    A. Hold the Jacks and 2s.
    B. Hold the Jacks.

2. **Ace of hearts, Ace of clubs, 2 of diamonds, 2 of spades, 8 of clubs:**

   A. Hold the Aces and 2s.
   B. Hold the Aces.

3. **Ace of hearts, Ace of clubs, Ace of diamonds, 2 of diamonds, 2 of spades:**

   A. Hold the full house.
   B. Hold only the Aces.

4. **Ace of hearts, Queen of spades, Jack of clubs, 6 of diamonds, 2 of diamonds:**

   A. Hold the Ace.
   B. Hold Ace-Queen-Jack.
   C. Hold Queen-Jack.

5. **Ace of hearts, Ace of diamonds, King of diamonds, Queen of diamonds, Jack of diamonds:**

   A: Hold the Aces.
   B. Hold the four-card royal flush.

6. **Queen of clubs, Jack of spades, 10 of hearts, 9 of diamonds, 3 of clubs:**

   A. Hold Queen-Jack.
   B. Hold Queen-Jack-10-9.

7. **Queen of clubs, Jack of spades, 9 of hearts, 8 of diamonds, 3 of clubs:**

   A. Hold Queen-Jack.
   B. Hold Queen-Jack-9-8.

8. **Jack of hearts, 9 of hearts, 6 of hearts, 3 of clubs, 2 of spades:**

   A. Hold the Jack.
   B. Hold the three-card flush.

9. **10 of hearts, 9 of hearts, 5 of hearts, 3 of clubs, 2 of spades:**

   A. Hold the three-card flush.
   B. Discard all five cards.

10. **Ace of clubs, Jack of clubs, 9 of clubs, 6 of hearts, 3 of spades:**

    A. Hold the Ace.
    B. Hold Ace-Jack.
    C. Hold the three-card flush.

11. **King of spades, Queen of spades, 7 of spades, 6 of hearts, 3 of diamonds:**

    A. Hold King-Queen.
    B. Hold the three-card flush.

12. **Jack of spades, 10 of spades, 6 of spades, 4 of hearts, 2 of clubs:**

    A. Hold the Jack.
    B. Hold Jack-10.
    C. Hold the three-card flush.

13. **9 of clubs, 8 of diamonds, 7 of hearts, 6 of spades, 6 of hearts:**

    A. Hold the pair of 6s.
    B. Hold 9-8-7 and one of the 6s.

14. **9 of clubs, 8 of diamonds, 6 of hearts, 5 of spades, 5 of hearts:**

    A. Hold the pair of 5s.
    B. Hold 9-8-6 and one of the 5s.

15. **9 of clubs, 8 of diamonds, 6 of hearts, 5 of spades, 2 of hearts:**

    A. Hold 9-8-6-5.
    B. Discard all five cards.

16. **Ace of spades, King of spades, King of diamonds, Jack of spades, 6 of spades.**

    A. Hold the pair of Kings.
    B. Hold the three-card royal.
    C. Hold all four spades.

17. **King of hearts, Queen of hearts, Jack of hearts, 9 of spades, 2 of hearts.**

    A. Hold the three-card royal.
    B. Hold all four hearts.
    C. Hold King-Queen-Jack-9.

18. **King of hearts, Queen of clubs, Jack of diamonds, 9 of spades, 2 of hearts.**

    A. Hold King-Queen-Jack.
    B. Hold King-Queen-Jack-9.

19. **Queen of clubs, 7 of diamonds, 6 of hearts, 5 of clubs, 3 of spades.**

    A. Hold the Queen.
    B. Hold 7-6-5-3.

20. **Jack of clubs, 10 of clubs, 8 of spades, 7 of spades, 4 of diamonds.**

    A. Hold the Jack.
    B. Hold Jack-10.
    C. Hold Jack-10-8-7.

Video Poker Hand Number 5: Double Bonus Poker Answers

1. A. Double Bonus Poker continually presents us with situations just a little different from those we see in Jacks or Better or Bonus Poker. This decision, whether to hold two pair or just the Jacks, would be obvious in games that pay 2-for-1 on two pair. It's less obvious here, where two pair pays the same 1-for-1 as a pair of Jacks, but we still hold both pairs. By holding both pairs, we have four chances in forty-seven at a full house. The expected value for holding both pairs is 8.83; for the Jacks alone, it's 7.29.

2. A. The big jackpot on four Aces makes this a close call, but it's still a slightly better play to hold both pairs and take the shot at a full house. The EVs are close—8.83 for the two pair, 8.82 on the Aces. So if jackpot hunters prefer to take their risks and give themselves a shot at an 800-coin payoff on four Aces, they're giving up little in the long run.

3. B. This play drew a lot of mail the first time I printed a Double Bonus strategy in my newspaper column. How can you give up a full house, especially one with a 50-coin payoff as in 10-7 Double Bonus Poker? Well, in the long run you'll hit four Aces enough times that breaking up the full house to hold three Aces is the better play. Holding just the Aces has an EV of 50.57. Holding the full house pays a flat 50. This is another marginal play. I'll not blame short-bankrolled players who want to hold on to the sure thing.

4. C. We play three high cards of mixed suits the same way we do it in Jacks or Better. When one of the cards is an Ace, hold the other two and ditch the Ace. What makes this an interesting hand is that some players, with an eye on the jackpot for four Aces, will just keep the Ace here. Sorry, the longshot at drawing three more Aces isn't worth it. The EVs are 2.35 for Queen-Jack, 2.23 for Ace-Queen-Jack and 2.21 for the Ace alone.

5. B. A pair of Aces is a nice place to start, with an EV here of 8.81. But it's nowhere near as nice as a four-card royal, with an EV of 93.83. For every five coins we wager in this situation, we'll get nearly 94 coins in payouts. If you get a shot at that big royal flush jackpot, you have to go for it.

6. B. Double Bonus Poker increases the payoff for straights to 5-for-1, and that heightens the value of four-card straights. Here, with two high cards that could be paired up for Jacks or Better payoffs, the EV of the four-card straight is 4.89, more than twice as good as the 2.30 on Queen-Jack.

7. B. That five-coin payoff on straights also heightens the value of inside straights. In regular Jacks or Better, we'd just hold Queen-Jack here. But in Double Bonus Poker, we draw to inside straights, even those that don't include high cards. The EV of Queen-Jack-9-8 is 2.77, compared with 2.34 for Queen-Jack.

8. B. Another difference between 10-7 Double Bonus and regular Jacks or Better is that we hold three card flushes. Jack-9-6 of hearts has an EV of 2.32 to 2.20 for the Jack alone.

9. A. Even without any high cards, three-card flushes are better than starting over. By holding 10-9-6 of hearts, in the long run we get back 1.82 coins of every five we bet. That beats discarding all five cards, with an EV of 1.65.

10. C. When there are high cards involved in 10-7 Double Bonus Poker, three-card flushes are better than holding the high cards alone. The EVs are 2.82 for Ace-Jack-9, 2.75 for Ace-Jack and 2.20 for the Ace alone. In Jacks or Better, we'd hold Ace-Jack and dump the 9.

11. A. King-Queen is a better start than Ace-Jack because it leaves open more straight possibilities. Here, we hold the two-card royal instead of the three-card flush. It's a close call, though. King-Queen of spades has an EV of 2.825 compared with 2.817 for King-Queen-7.

12. B. The EVs are lower because we're eliminating some high pair possibilities, but a two-card royal with Jack-10 is still a better play than a three-card flush. EVs are 2.40 for Jack-10, 2.32 for Jack-10-6 and 2.17 for the Jack alone.

13. B. Those who checked out the Jacks or Better answers know that in that game we keep a low pair over a four-card straight. Not in Double Bonus. The 5-for-1 payoff on straights heightens the value of four-card straights, and the 1-for-1 payoff on two pair lowers the value of low pairs. The EVs here are 4.26 on the four-card straight, and 3.72 on the pair of 6s.

14. A. Low pairs are still better than inside straights in Double Bonus, although we do keep inside straights if nothing better is available. EVs are 3.72 for the low pair, 2.13 on the inside straight.

15. A. Here's where we keep the inside straight with no high cards. EV is 2.13 for the inside straight, 1.65 for just tossing them all away.

16. C. Breaking up a winning hand for a four-card flush is something we'd never do in regular Jacks or Better. But the heightened value of the flush—a 7-for-1 payoff—finds us keeping a lot of same-suit cards in 10-7 Double Bonus as well as in 9-7 Double Bonus. The EV is 7.55 on the four spades, 7.28 on the pair of Kings and 6.85 on the three-card royal. In Jacks or Better, we'd keep the Kings.

17. B. Even with the three-card royal having consecutive cards and no Ace to interfere with straights, the four-card flush is the better play. The EV is 7.66 on the four hearts, 7.49 on the three-card royal. The four-card inside straight, at 3.08, isn't in the same class as the other possibilities.

18. B. When the three high cards are of mixed suits, the inside straight becomes a viable alternative. The EV of 3.08 for the four-card inside straight bests the 2.51 for the three high cards.

19. A. When there are no high cards in a four-card inside straight, its entire value rests in the possibility of hitting the straight and the 5-for-1 payoffs. Better to start with the single Queen, EV of 2.22, than the low inside straight, 2.13.

20. C. With one high card, meaning there are high pair possibilities, the inside straight has an EV of 2.45. That's enough to push it past the 2.44 for the two-card royal and the 2.18 of the lone Jack. In regular Jacks or Better, we'd hold Jack-10 of clubs instead.

Video Poker Hand Number 6: Joker Poker

It's just one card out of fifty-three, but adding a Joker to the deck changes odds pretty dramatically. It can substitute for any card, and it makes it possible to hit five of a kind. There are more flushes and straights in Joker Poker than in regular Jacks or Better, and you have to be on the lookout for possible straight flushes.

The twenty problems that follow are based on the highest-paying available version of Joker Poker. Assuming five coins played—making you eligible for the big jackpot on a royal flush—it pays 800-for-1 for a natural royal, 200-for-1 for five of a kind, 100-for-1 for a royal flush that includes a Joker, 50-for-1 for a straight flush, 20-for-1 for four of a kind, 7-for-1 for a full house, 5-for-1 for a flush, 3-for-1 for a straight, 2-for-1 for three of a kind, 1-for-1 for two pair and 1-for-1 for a pair of Kings or Aces. With expert play, this machine returns 100.6 percent.

1. **King of hearts, Queen of diamonds, 7 of spades, 5 of clubs, 3 of hearts:**

    A. Hold the King.
    B. Hold King-Queen.

2. **King of hearts, Queen of hearts, 7 of spades, 5 of clubs, 3 of hearts:**

    A. Hold the King.
    B. Hold King-Queen.

3. **Ace of diamonds, King of hearts, 7 of spades, 5 of clubs, 3 of hearts:**

   A. Hold the King.
   B. Hold Ace-King.

4. **Ace of diamonds, King of hearts, 7 of hearts, 5 of hearts, 3 of hearts:**

   A. Hold the King.
   B. Hold Ace-King.
   C. Hold the four hearts.

5. **King of hearts, King of diamonds, Queen of diamonds, Jack of diamonds, 7 of clubs.**

   A. Hold the pair of Kings.
   B. Hold King-Queen-Jack of diamonds.

6. **8 of diamonds, 7 of diamonds, 6 of hearts, 5 of diamonds, 4 of diamonds.**

   A. Hold the straight.
   B. Hold the four diamonds.

7. **Queen of clubs, Jack of spades, 6 of hearts, 5 of diamonds, 4 of diamonds.**

   A. Hold Queen-Jack.
   B. Hold 4-5-6.
   C. Discard all five cards.

8. **Queen of clubs, Jack of clubs, 6 of hearts, 5 of diamonds, 4 of diamonds.**

   A. Hold Queen-Jack.
   B. Hold 4-5-6.
   C. Discard all five cards.

9. **Queen of clubs, Jack of spades, 6 of hearts, 5 of hearts, 2 of hearts.**

   A. Hold Queen-Jack.
   B. Hold 2-5-6.

C. Discard all five cards.

10. **Ace of spades, Ace of diamonds, Queen of hearts, Jack of hearts, 10 of hearts.**

    A. Hold the pair of Aces.
    B. Hold Queen-Jack-10.

11. **Joker, 3 of clubs, 5 of hearts, 7 of diamonds, 9 of spades.**

    A. Hold the Joker.
    B. Hold Joker-9.

12. **Joker, Queen of diamonds, Jack of diamonds, 10 of diamonds, King of clubs.**

    A. Hold the straight.
    B. Hold Joker-King
    C. Hold the four-card royal.

13. **Joker, 4 of spades, 5 of spades, 3 of diamonds, 3 of spades.**

    A. Hold Joker-3-3.
    B. Hold Joker and the three spades.

14. **Joker, King of hearts, Queen of hearts, 10 of hearts, 5 of hearts.**

    A. Hold the flush.
    B. Hold Joker-King-Queen-10.

15. **Joker, 8 of hearts, 7 of spades, 6 of hearts, 2 of hearts.**

    A. Hold Joker-8-6-2.
    B. Hold Joker-8-7-6.
    C. Hold Joker-8-6.

16. **Joker, Ace of spades, 9 of clubs, 8 of clubs, 4 of diamonds.**

    A. Hold Joker-Ace.
    B. Hold Joker-9-8.

17. **Joker, Ace of spades, 10 of spades, 8 of spades, 4 of diamonds.**

A. Hold Joker-Ace.

B. Hold Joker Ace-10.

C. Hold Joker-Ace-10-8.

18. **Joker, 10 of hearts, 9 of hearts, 8 of spades, 7 of hearts.**

A. Hold Joker-10-9-8-7.

B. Hold Joker 10-9-7.

19. **Joker, Queen of hearts, Jack of hearts, 10 of hearts, 9 of hearts.**

A. Hold Joker-Queen-Jack-10-9.

B. Hold Joker-Queen-Jack-10.

20. **Joker, King of hearts, Jack of spades, 10 of spades, 7 of spades.**

A. Hold Joker-King.

B. Hold Joker-Jack-10.

C. Hold Joker-Jack-10-7.

Video Poker Hand Number 6: Joker Poker Answers

1. A. With the Kings or better pay table, a Queen or a Jack is just another low card. Pairing up the Queen here wouldn't give us any payback, so there is no value to keeping it. The expected value of keeping just the King is 2.27; for King-Queen, it's 1.75.

If you play Joker Poker with a pay table that starts at two pair or better, the Aces and Kings also have no more value than any other card. With this hand in a two pair or better game, we'd discard all five cards.

2. B. It's a different story from number 1 when both the King and Queen are of the same suit. Now we open possible big payoffs for a royal flush or wild royal, with other straight flushes, flushes and straights also possible. In what's still a fairly close call, we hold the King-Queen of hearts, with an EV of 2.32, instead of just the King, at 2.21.

3. B. Just as in Jacks or Better, we hold two high cards when available. It's a closer call in Joker Poker than in Jacks or Better, though, largely because holding two cards of different denominations takes us out of the running for five of a kind. The EV for Ace-King is 2.27, to 2.22 for the lone King.

4. C. This is essentially the same hand as number 3, except that the three low cards are all the same suit as the King. The four-card flush, with an EV of 5.52, in the long run will pay us more than the five coins per hand we put into the machine. That dwarfs any possibilities from holding just King or Ace-King.

5. B. With the Joker thrown into the mix, we break up winning hands for royal flush possibilities a little earlier than in Jacks or Better. In Jacks or Better, we'd need a four-card royal or four-card straight flush before breaking up a winning high pair. Here, a three-card royal is good enough. The EV for King-Queen-Jack is 7.19. For the pair of Kings, it's 7.00.

6. B. This is another hand that's played differently in Joker Poker than in regular Jacks or Better. There are two things at work. The straight here pays only 15 coins for 5 played instead of the 20 you'd get back in Jacks or Better. Also, the Joker gives us an extra card to complete the inside straight flush. You could settle for the flat payout of 15 coins for holding the straight, but the EV of going for the straight flush is 15.21.

7. C. The best value here is to start all over. Since we can't get a payoff by simply pairing up the Queen or Jack, anything we hold here would require us to draw at least two helpful cards to make a winning hand. The EV of dumping all five cards is 1.65, a fair distance ahead of the 1.22 of holding the three-card straight or the 1.10 on the Jack-Queen. Actually, the second-best play in this hand with an EV of 1.50 is to hold the Jack by itself. That's not good enough. Discard the whole hand.

8. A. When the Queen-Jack are the same suit, that's just enough to nudge it ahead of discarding all five cards. The EV is still low—for every five coins you play in this situation, you'll get back 1.79 by holding Queen-Jack. That's not great, but it's better than chucking the whole thing (EV 1.66).

9. B. The 2-5-6 of hearts could turn into a straight flush with any two of three cards—Joker, 3 of hearts, 4 of hearts. There are also other straight and flush possibilities. That makes B by far the best option here, with an EV of 2.46.

10. B. Even with no high cards, the three-card royal is a better play than holding a high pair. Here, Queen-Jack-10 has an EV of 7.32, while the pair of Aces checks in at 7.00. The Joker gives us extra shots at straights, flushes and straight flushes and an opportunity to hit a pretty good payoff on a wild royal if we miss the big one on the natural royal.

11. B. One thing that makes Joker Poker a much different game than the other wild-card standard, Deuces Wild, is that we hold a middling card—a 5 through 10 that leaves open lots of straight and straight flush possibilities—instead of just holding a lone Joker. Here, the EV of holding Joker-9 is 7.36, better than the 7.12 for the Joker alone.

12. C. We have two pre-draw winners here with a straight or a pair of Kings, but we break them both up. Joker with Queen-Jack-10 in the same suit leaves us with a one-card draw in which either of two cards complete the wild royal. Either the Ace or King of diamonds will do. Either the 8 or 9 of diamonds gives us a straight flush. There are six other diamonds to complete a flush, and any King or Ace would pair up with the Joker for a high-pair winner. That yields an EV of 39.69, compared with 8.43 for Joker-King and a flat payout of 15 coins for holding the straight.

13. B. Any of four cards complete a straight flush—Ace, 2, 6 or 7 of spades. That's too good a chance to pass up, even if it means busting up three of a kind. The EV on Joker plus the three spades is 29.69; on holding the three of a kind it's 19.68.

14. B. Take a chance on the four-card wild royal. In the long run, you'll get back 36.04 coins for every five you play. Holding the flush yields a flat 25-coin payoff for five played.

15. C. When trying to decide between the four-card straight or the four-card flush, don't overlook the three-card straight flush. That's the best play here, with an EV of 8.56 to 7.71 for either the four-card flush or the four-card straight. How can the flush and straight draws be equal when the flush pays so much more? Well, there are more ways to make the straights. There are ten cards that would complete the flush, but there are sixteen that would complete the straight—any of the 10s, 9s, 5s or 4s in the deck. The average winning hand will pay more with the flush draw, but there will be more winning hands with the draw to the straight.

16. B. The three-card straight flush makes it worth breaking up the winning pair. Joker-9-8 has an EV of 9.44 compared with 8.57 for Joker-Ace.

17. C. The one-card draw to a flush beats the other options. Even with no straight flush available, the EV of 10.10 beats the 9.59 for the three-card royal (Joker-Ace-10) and 8.57 for Joker-Ace.

18. B. You can play conservatively and take the 15-coin pay-off on a straight, or you can take a shot at the inside straight flush. That's actually the better play. You'll get back 24.27 coins for every five played by going for the inside straight flush instead of settling for the 15 on the straight.

19. A. Even with a four-card natural royal, we'd defer to the pat straight flush. Here, where we'd be going for wild royal with its lower return, it's no contest. We take the flat 250-coin payoff on the straight flush instead of the EV of 34.79 on the four-card wild royal.

20. C. As you've no doubt noticed by now, we like partial straight flushes in this game, even when they require inside draws. The four-card straight flush, with an EV of 18.15, beats the pair of Kings hands down, with an EV of 8.47. Holding Joker-Jack-10, a three-card wild royal, is a little better than just holding the Kings, but its EV of 9.04 is no match for the inside straight flush.

Video Poker Hand Number 7: Deuces Wild

Whenever I'm in Las Vegas I save some time for full-pay Deuces Wild. It's as different as you can get from Jacks or Better, and to get the most out of it requires learning a whole new strategy. If you don't get your share of deuces, you're in trouble. But when the deuces are coming your way, you'll swear this is more than a 100.7 percent machine.

Different Deuces Wild pay tables have their own little quirks that may require strategy adjustments. But this is the machine you should be seeking out. I generally save my Deuces play for Nevada.

If you know the right way to play these 20 hands, you're ready to tackle full-pay Deuces Wild, which pays 800-for-1 on a natural royal flush, 200-for-1 on four deuces, 25-for-1 on a royal flush with wild cards, 15-for-1 on five of a kind, 9-for-1 on a straight flush, 5-for-1 on four of a kind, 3-for-1 on a full house, 2-for-1 on a flush, 2-for-1 on a straight and 1-for-1 on three of a kind:

1. **King of clubs, 10 of diamonds, 8 of hearts 6 of spades, 6 of clubs.**

   A. Hold the 6s.
   B. Hold the King.

2. **King of spades, 10 of spades, 8 of spades, 6 of spades, 6 of clubs.**

    A. Hold the 6s.

    B. Hold King-10.

    C. Hold all four spades.

3. **King of clubs, Queen of clubs, Jack of clubs, 10 of clubs, 9 of clubs.**

    A. Hold the straight flush.

    B. Hold King-Queen-Jack-10.

4. **King of diamonds, Jack of diamonds, 10 of diamonds, 9 of diamonds, 5 of diamonds.**

    A. Hold the flush.

    B. Hold King-Jack-10.

    C. Hold King-Jack-10-9.

5. **Ace of diamonds, Queen of clubs, 10 of diamonds, 8 of diamonds, 3 of spades.**

    A. Hold Ace-10.

    B. Hold all three diamonds.

    C. Discard all five cards.

6. **Jack of hearts, 9 of diamonds, 9 of hearts, 6 of spades, 6 of clubs.**

    A. Hold the 6s.

    B. Hold the 9s.

    C. Hold the 6s and 9s.

7. **Deuce of hearts, 8 of hearts, 7 of hearts, 6 of spades, 6 of clubs.**

    A. Hold 2-6-6.

    B. Hold 2-6-7-8 of hearts.

8. **Deuce of hearts, Queen of spades, Jack of spades, 8 of hearts, 6 of diamonds.**

    A. Hold only the 2.

    B. Hold 2-Queen-Jack.

9. **Deuce of hearts, Queen of spades, Jack of spades, 8 of spades, 6 of diamonds.**

   A. Hold only the 2.
   B. Hold 2-Queen-Jack.
   C. Hold 2-Queen-Jack-8

10. **Deuce of hearts, Queen of spades, 8 of spades, 7 of spades, 6 of diamonds.**

   A. Hold only the 2.
   B. Hold the 2 plus the three spades.
   C. Hold 2-7-8.

11. **Deuce of hearts, 9 of spades, 8 of spades, 7 of spades, 3 of clubs.**

   A. Hold only the 2.
   B. Hold the 2 plus the three spades.

12. **Deuce of hearts, deuce of spades, King of diamonds, 10 of clubs, 4 of clubs.**

   A. Hold 2-2.
   B. Hold 2-2-King.

13. **Deuce of hearts, deuce of spades, King of diamonds, 10 of diamonds, 4 of clubs.**

   A. Hold 2-2.
   B. Hold 2-2-King-10.

14. **Deuce of hearts, Deuce of spades, King of diamonds, 9 of diamonds, 4 of diamonds.**

   A. Hold 2-2.
   B. Hold the flush.

15. **Deuce of hearts, Deuce of spades, 9 of diamonds, 8 of diamonds, 4 of spades.**

   A. Hold 2-2.
   B. Hold 2-2-9-8.

16. **Deuce of hearts, Deuce of spades, Deuce of diamonds, 9 of diamonds, 3 of diamonds.**

> A. Hold 2-2-2.
> B. Hold 2-2-2-9.
> C. Hold 2-2-2-9-3.

17. **Deuce of hearts, Deuce of spades, Deuce of diamonds, 9 of diamonds, 8 of diamonds.**

> A. Hold 2-2-2.
> B. Hold the straight flush.

18. **Deuce of hearts, Deuce of spades, Deuce of diamonds, King of diamonds, 8 of clubs.**

> A. Hold 2-2-2.
> B. Hold 2-2-2-K.

19. **Deuce of hearts, Deuce of spades, Deuce of diamonds, 5 of hearts, 5 of spades.**

> A. Hold 2-2-2.
> B. Hold 2-2-2-10-10.

20. **Deuce of hearts, Deuce of spades, Deuce of diamonds, Deuce of clubs, 4 of clubs.**

> A. Hold 2-2-2-2.
> B. Hold 2-2-2-2-4.

Video Poker
Hand Number 7:
Deuces Wild
Answers

1. A. With payoffs beginning at three of a kind, the rank of a single card means very little in Deuces Wild. A King is no better a starting point than a 7—a bit worse, in fact, because the 7 leaves open more straight possibilities. A pair, on the other hand, is a pretty good way to start. Add a deuce or two or three, and a pair has big possibilities. The expected value here is 2.73 on the pair of 6s—in the long run, you'll get 2.73 coins back for every five you bet on this hand. The EV on the King is 1.28—worse than just tossing the whole hand away.

2. A. There are times to go for two-card royals, and times to hold four-card flushes. This isn't one of them. The pair of 6s is flat-out stronger than the four-card flush. The most the four-flush could become is a flush paying 10 coins for 5 played. The pair has many more possibilities—three of a kind, full house, four of a kind, five of a kind. That shows up in the EVs of 2.80 for the pair and 2.55 for the four-card flush. The two-card royal is weakened by having two other spades in the hand. In order to draw to King-10, we'd have to reduce our flush chances by discarding the 6 and 8 of spades. Even if there weren't stronger possibilities in the hand—and a pair is always stronger than a two-card royal—we'd hold King-10 suited only if none of the discards interfered with possible flushes or straights.

3. B. It's tempting just to hold the straight flush and take the 45-coin payout. Those weaned on Jacks or Better know to hold the straight flush, but in Jacks or Better it's worth a 250-coin jack-pot for five played. In full-pay Deuces, it's only 45 coins, and we have a hand that give us loads of possibilities. Just as in other games, we have 1 in 47 shot at hitting the Ace of clubs for a 4,000-coin payday. But here, we also have four wild deuces, any of which would give us a wild royal for 125 coins. Barring the big hits, we could still get a little something with flush and straight possibilities. That gives us an expected value of 98.30 on the four-card royal, outweighing the 45-coin payoff on the straight flush.

4. A. With only three cards to a royal, we're better off taking the sure payoff. We get 10 coins for five played by holding the flush. EVs are 6.70 on the four-card straight flush and 6.48 on the three-card royal.

5. C. We don't hold two-card royals that include an Ace. The Ace limits possible straights, giving us fewer potential payoffs for the large majority of hands that we don't hit the royal. We don't hold three-card flushes in Deuces Wild, either. Those forty-seven remaining undealt cards include four wild cards. Better to take a blind chance than to stay with a hand with limited possibilities. The EVS are 1.62 for dumping all five cards, 1.41 for holding Ace-10 and a mere 0.93 for holding the three diamonds.

6. A or B. It doesn't matter which pair you hold. In the long run, you'll get back 2.81 coins for every five you bet. Better to take the chance on three, four or five of a kind than to hold both pairs, yielding a shot at nothing more than a full house that pays only 3-for-1. The EV of holding both pairs is 2.55.

In Deuces Wild versions that lower the four-of-a-kind payoff to 4-for-1 and raise full houses to 4-for-1, we reverse this play. In those versions, it's worthwhile holding both pairs and taking the 8-in-47 chance on a full house.

7. A. Hold the paying hand, three of a kind, rather than tak-ing a chance on a one-card draw for a straight. Straights are com-mon in Deuces Wild. At about one straight per 16 hands, they occur more than five times as frequently as in Jacks or Better. But straights pay only 2-for-1 in this game. Better to take the sure 1-for-1 on three of a kind and hope it develops into something better. EVs are 10.09 for 2-6-6 and 4.89 for 2-8-7-6.

8. B. A lone deuce is a pretty good way to start a hand. If we started every hand with a 2 and four garbage cards, holding only the 2, we'd make a profit in the long run. The EV on the single 2 here is 5.15—we get back an average of 5.15 coins for every 5 we bet. But wild royal flushes occur frequently enough that 2-Queen-Jack is an even stronger start, with an EV of 6.11.

9. C. Watch for inside straight flushes. That's what we have here in C. Any one card of the remaining three deuces, the 9 of spades or 10 of spades will give us a straight flush. The EV is 8.51, compared with 5.87 on 2-Queen-Jack and 5.16 on the lone 2.

10. C. The three-card straight flush, with an EV of 5.31, is a slightly better play than just holding the 2, with an EV of 5.16. We do not hold four-card flushes in hands that include a 2. There must be straight flush possibilities before those cards are worthy of standing beside our deuce. The EV of 3.51 is acceptable in no-deuce hands, but once there's a deuce in the hand, it's just not good enough. The deuce is stronger on its own.

11. B. This is more like it. There's not only a possible straight flush, it's open on both ends. Lots of cards will complete this one for a 45-coin payout—any of the remaining three 2s or the 5, 6, 10 or Jack of spades. The EV of 11.28 on the four-card straight flush is more than double the 5.18 on the 2 alone.

12. A. With two deuces, we hold the 2s alone a lot. If we don't have at least four of a kind, or one-card draws to royal flushes or straight flushes, we're better off with just the 2s. Even adding a royal flush card like the King of diamonds doesn't change that. The two 2s in the long run will bring us 16.23 coins for every five we play; 2-2-King will bring only 13.81.

13. B. With two royal flush cards to go with our two 2s, we have something to shoot for. Now either of the other two 2s, or the Ace, Queen or Jack of diamonds, will bring us a wild royal for a 125-coin payout. We can also hit a straight flush with the 9 of diamonds. The EV is 23.08 on 2-2-King-10, 16.31 on just the 2s.

14. A. The flush brings us only a 10-coin return. Why settle for that when our average return starting with two 2s is 16.32. That includes a five-coin mimimum return. With two wild cards, we'll never have less than three of a kind.

15. B. By a narrow margin, the four-card straight flush is a keeper. We have lots of ways to make the straight flush—any card out of the other two 2s, the 6, 7, 10 or Jack of diamonds. That gives us an EV of 16.70 for the four-card straight flush to 16.32 for the deuces alone.

16. A. I include this specific hand because an onlooker asked me once why I was breaking up a flush by throwing away the 9 and 3 of diamonds. If I'd held all the cards, it still wouldn't have been a flush, it would have been four of a kind with a 25-coin payoff. Discard both cards, and the three wild cards mean you still wind up with at least four of a kind.

Three-deuce hands are powerhouses. Here's where we hit most of our wild royals and fives of a kind, and where we get two shots among the remaining forty-seven cards of drawing that fourth deuce for a 1,000-coin jackpot. The EV on three 2s alone is 75. Don't water it down by settling for a lesser hand.

17. A. Even a straight flush is a lesser hand than you should accept when you start with three deuces. Go for the big hands. Don't settle for a 45-coin payout. You have at least 25 in hand for your four of a kind. See if you can draw the fourth 2 and get 1,000.

18. A. Four to a wild royal is a pretty good hand—better than a pat straight flush. It has an EV of 57.87. Still not good enough. Go for the deuces.

19. B. OK, with five of a kind, you can take your flat 75-coin payoff. Same with five Jacks, Queens, Kings or Aces. But if we had three Deuces with two 3s through 9s, we'd just hold the Deuces. Holding five of a kind vs. three Deuces is a borderline play, and the presence of a royal flush card pushes us over the edge. If our five of a kind is 10s or higher, our chances of hitting a wild royal flush are decreased just enough tht the best bet is to hold the quints. But with 9s or lower, all the royal flush cards remain as possible draws, and it's a better play just to hold the three Deuces.

20. B. Either way, you're going to get your 1,000-coin jackpot for four deuces. Unless, that is, there's a one-in-a-zillion malfunction. Let's say you hold only the four 2s, hit the draw button, and another 2 pops up in a program malfunction. The casino can deny you your jackpot in the case of malfunctions, and the presence of five 2s on the screen would make it pretty obvious there was something wrong.

You'll probably never see this happen, but why take chances? Hold all five cards.

Roulette
Spin Number 1:
Getting Started

No full-service casino is complete without roulette. In the United States, it's not the popular favorite that blackjack is now, craps was a couple of generations ago, or faro a couple of generations before that, but sooner or later everyone tries their lucky numbers at roulette, a venerable game that remains a favorite of systems players. See how much you know about how roulette came to be a casino standard.

1. **Roulette in its modern form dates back to:**

    A. Monaco in the 1600s.
    B. France in the 1700s.
    C. Belgium in the 1800s.

2. **One of roulette's predecessors was an English game called:**

    A. Roly-poly.
    B. 36-and-out.
    C. Rouge et noir.

3. **The key invention that made roulette possible was:**

    A. The ivory ball.
    B. Varnish.
    C. The horizontal gaming wheel.

4. Compared with the popularity of roulette in the United States, the game is:

    A. More popular in Europe.

    B. Less popular in Europe.

    C. About as popular in Europe.

5. Among table games in the United States, roulette's popularity ranks:

    A. Second.

    B. Third.

    C. Fourth.

6. The most important difference between American and European roulette is:

    A. There are more bets available in Europe.

    B. The U.S. wheel is more finely balanced.

    C. The European wheel does not have 00.

7. One bet commonly available in the United States not available in Europe is:

    A. 9-number quadrants.

    B. Five-number.

    C. 12-number columns.

8. The base inside which the roulette wheel spins is called the:

    A. Bowl.

    B. Apron.

    C. Pit.

9. The metal pieces that separate numbers on the wheel are called:

    A. Dividers.

    B. Barriers.

    C. Frets.

10. An American roulette wheel has:

  A. 36 numbers.
  B. 37 numbers.
  C. 38 numbers.

11. A European roulette wheel has:

  A. 36 numbers.
  B. 37 numbers.
  C. 38 numbers.

12. In roulette lore, English engineer Joseph Jaggers is famous for:

  A. Breaking the bank at Monte Carlo.
  B. Inventing the roulette wheel.
  C. Introducing roulette to the United States.

13. The table layout on which players place their bets:

  A. Has numbers in the same order as the wheel.
  B. Has numbers in reverse order of the wheel.
  C. Has numbers in numerical order.

14. The wheel has numbers arranged:

  A. So that numbers are approximately opposite each other.
  B. In numerical order.
  C. In numerical order, except that 0 and 00 are opposite each other.

15. When the dealer lets go of the ball:

  A. Players must cease betting.
  B. Betting may begin.
  C. Players may continue betting until the ball starts its descent.

16. When the ball stops on a number, the dealer immediately:

  A. Pays off all winners.
  B. Sweeps off all losing bets.
  C. Places a marker on the winning number.

17. Players may begin betting:

A. When the dealer has taken the marker off the layout.
B. Once they've been paid.
C. When the dealer lets go of the ball.

18. Roulette players usually bet using:

A. Regular casino chips.
B. Special roulette chips, with each player getting his own color.
C. Cash.

19. At the roulette table, roulette chips have a value:

A. Of $1 each.
B. Of $5 each.
C. Determined when you buy them.

20. At the cashier's cage, roulette chips have a value of:

A. Zero.
B. $1 each.
C. $5 each.

Roulette
Spin Number 1:
Getting Started
Answers

1. B. Modern roulette wheels have been traced to Paris in 1796. All the elements of today's game are intact: alternating red and black slots, numbers 1 through 36 with both zero and double-zero. The double-zero was later dropped from the standard European wheel.

Just a few years earlier, French wheels alternated red and black slots, but were not numbered. Russell T. Barnhart, in his excellent book *Beating the Wheel*, speculates that the 36-number version of the Italian ball game biribi, then popular in France, was adapted to the existing wheel.

2. A. Roly-poly, introduced in England in 1720, alternated black slots and white slots, and players bet on either black or white. There were also a bar white slot and a bar black slot. All bets lost on either of the bar slots, giving the operator an advantage in the game.

3. C. The horizontal gaming wheel was invented for roly-poly in 1720. Roly-poly itself was banned in England in 1745, but the wheel has proved remarkably enduring. In the relatively short time to 1796, the version of roulette that has survived intact for more than 200 years has been played on that wheel.

4. A. Roulette seems almost an afterthought in American casinos. The player must work his way around hundreds, if not thousands, of slot machines and dozens of blackjack tables to find a roulette wheel or two. Some states don't even allow roulette. Native American casinos in Wisconsin, for example, have slots, video poker and blackjack, but no craps or roulette.

In Europe, roulette is a much more important part of the mix. Part of that is historical and cultural. Roulette has been around in Europe for more than 200 years, and has remained a favorite across generations of players. European casinos also are not designed to be entertainment for the masses. They are meant for the upper crust and for travelers. Much less floor space is devoted to slot machines, and in many casinos the relative handful of slots are shunted to a separate room away from the elegant atmosphere of the tables. In that atmosphere, roulette's place is front and center.

Even without the historical and cultural trappings, European roulette has a big edge on the American version. It has a much lower house edge, and gives the player a better run for his money. Just how big that edge is and how it's derived are subjects for more questions in *Roulette Spin Number 3: Bets and Percentages.*

5. B. In number of players, roulette is a distant third in the United States behind blackjack and craps. In terms of money wagered, it also ranks behind baccarat in the traditional gaming states of Nevada and New Jersey. Baccarat is the game of choice for many super-high rollers, and one billionaire on a spree can balance off a whole bunch of roulette players.

In some newer gaming jurisdictions, roulette is being pushed and even surpassed for the number 3 spot among table games by Caribbean Stud Poker. In 1996, for example, casino revenues from Caribbean Stud outstripped those at roulette at seven of Illinois' ten casino operations.

6. C. The standard European wheel has only a 0, with no 00. The standard American wheel has both 0 and 00. However, there are double-zero wheels in Europe and there are a few single-zero wheels in the United States. The Monte Carlo casino on the Las Vegas Strip, with its European theme, has single-zero roulette. Single-zero wheels also show up in the competitive markets of Mississippi.

7. B. On an American wheel, the player can bet the five-number combination of 0, 00, 1, 2 and 3. The table layout is arranged with 0 and 00 at the top, with twelve rows of three numbers each underneath. So the five-number bet is the 0 and 00 together with the first row. Winning five-number bets pays 6-1.

There are no five-number bets on a single-zero layout. The player can bet the first four combination of 0, 1, 2 and 3. It pays the same 8-1 as on any other four-number combination.

8. A. The wheel head, which is the part containing the numbers, sits in the bowl. A hole in the center of the wheel head slides over a spindle in the center of the bowl. The turret then fits over the spindle to hold everything together. There's a lot more hardware involved, but these are the raw basics of how the major wheel parts fit together.

9. C. The barriers between numbers are called frets, just like the barriers between notes on your guitar or ukulele.

10. C. The American wheel has 38 numbers: 1 through 36, plus 0 and 00.

Players sometimes forget the 0 and 00 count as numbers. A few years ago I was playing in a charity casino, knowing full well I was really donating a few dollars to the local Lions Club. The ball landed in double-zero, and the Lion running the game swept all the chips off the layout like an old pro.

One of the other players shook his head and moaned, "What are the odds of THAT?"

I smiled and said, "The same as on any other number."

A quizzical expression came over his face, then he relaxed and replied, "I never thought of that, but that's exactly right. The odds are the same as any other number."

With 38 numbers on an American wheel, that makes the odds of any number hitting on a particular spin 37-1. The house pays winners at 35-1. You can see why the house makes money.

11. B. There are 37 numbers on a European wheel, 1 through 36 and 0. That makes the odds of any given number showing up 36-1. The house still pays 35-1.

12. A. In 1873, Joseph Jaggers went on a run at the Beaux Arts Monte Carlo casino that not only made him a tidy sum, it forced the casino to reinvent the wheel.

Jaggers, an engineer and mechanic in the cotton industry hired six clerks to record every number that came up on the casino's six roulette wheels in the twelve hours a day the casino was open. He then stayed in his room for most of six days, analyzing statistics with pencil and paper in those days long before invention of the computer. The numbers told Jaggers that the numbers 7, 8, 9, 17, 18, 19, 22, 28 and 29 were hitting more often than they should by chance. He took that knowledge to the casino, and won roughly $70,000 on his first night of serious play. By the fourth day, his winnings pushed $300,000, and other casino patrons crowded in to bet the same numbers.

Beaux-Arts couldn't let this go on, so overnight, employees rearranged the wheels, each going to a different table. When Jaggers sat down the next morning, he was at the same table, but a different wheel was in its place. But after a losing streak, Jaggers realized that a small scratch that he'd noticed on his winning wheel wasn't there. He checked the other tables, found the biased wheel and resumed winning. He not only recovered his losses, he pushed his total winnings to $450,000, and for 1873, that was an astronomical sum.

The casino finally put a stop to Jaggers' streak by having its wheel manufacturer in Paris design a set of movable frets. Each night after closing, the frets would be moved to new locations around the wheel. Jaggers went on a two-day losing streak, and called it quits with $325,000 in profits. He never returned to Monte Carlo.

Other players have been trying to find biased wheels ever since, but to be mathematically certain that the effect is real and not a normal fluctuation due to random chance involves charting thousands of spins. The number-crunching could be done with a computer now instead of pencil and paper, but it still would take three or four days of round-the-clock charting to get a large enough sample to be sure. That doesn't mean such charting doesn't happen—it does—but it requires enormous time and patience with no guarantee of reward.

13. C. The table layout has the numbers in numerical order. Zero and double-zero are at the top, followed by a row of 1, 2 and 3, then 4, 5 and 6, and so on until twelve rows of three take us through number 36.

14. A. It's not perfect, but the attempt was made to place consecutive numbers opposite each other. Check out the numbers around 0 and 00. Zero is flanked by 2 and 28; on either side of 00 are 1 and 27. Basically, odd numbers are placed directly opposite the next higher even number.

15. C. Players may continue betting until the ball's rotation starts to decay and it begins falling toward the numbered slots. At that point, the dealer will call "No more bets."

The dealer has to be alert at this point for an illegal practice called "past posting." Cheaters sometimes try this at a noisy, busy table, when the dealer is distracted looking to see in which numbered slot the ball has landed. The player may try to spot the number first and slip an extra bet on the table, or a partner stationed near the wheel may signal the number to a bettor farther down the table. I've seen a security tape in which one partner signalled to the other that the number was in the second column. When the dealer looked up, there was a $100 bet on the second column she hadn't noticed before.

It's risky business. Past posting and other forms of cheating the casino are felonies in most gaming states.

16. C. The dealer first places a marker on the winning number. If there are single-number bets on the winner, the marker goes on top of the bets. Then the dealer sweeps all the losing bets off the layout. She next pays winning bets on the outside propositions—red/black, odd/even, first 36/last 36, dozens or columns—by placing chips next to the original bets. Finally, the inside bets on the numbers themselves are paid. The dealer places the winnings in front of the player, on the table but off the betting layout, while leaving the original wager on the table. After the dealer removes the marker, the player may remove those bets, but should he wish to play the same numbers again, they're in place.

17. A. Players must wait to bet until the dealer removes the marker, signifying that she has paid all winning bets and collected all losers and is ready to move on to the next spin.

I got caught up in this little piece of etiquette one of the first times I played without even realizing what I was doing. I had several winning bets in a row on black, and each time I removed my winnings from the layout and left my original bet up before the dealer had removed the marker. She rebuked me a couple of times for betting early. I didn't even realize I WAS betting early. I thought I was just collecting my winnings.

A little later, a dealer trainee came on, and our original dealer supervised while he made payouts. Being unusually dense that day, I did the same thing: as soon as I was paid, I picked up my winnings and left my original bet on the table for the next spin. The trainee looked away to pay any bets, but when he looked back and saw a single stack of chips on black with no winnings next to it, he was confused.

"I could have sworn I paid that off," he said.

The original dealer piped in, "You did. This has become a war of nerves between him and me."

It finally dawned on me just what the problem was. I no longer pick up my winnings early while leaving the bet on the table.

18. B. Players can use regular casino chips, and in some jurisdictions can even play with cash. But most commonly, players use special roulette chips. Each player at the table gets his own color. With just one betting layout and several players often making the same bet, that helps keep track of just whose bet is whose. At most casinos, even couples obviously together are not allowed to share a color. If both are betting, each must have a separate color.

19. C. One color of roulette chip can have several different values over the course of a day. Let's say I buy in for $10, and tell the dealer I want 25-cent chips. He has light blue chips available, so he gives me forty light blues, places one on a rail next to the wheel and places a marker atop that chip indicating that color is worth 25 cents per chip. Later, when I leave the table, I give the dealer any roulette chips I have left, and he exchanges for regular casino chips, which I may then cash in at the cashier's cage.

My place at the table is immediately taken by a wealthier sort, who puts $200 on the table and says he wants $5 chips. Light blue has been freed up, so the dealer gives the player forty light blue chips, then puts a $5 marker atop a light blue chip on the real. When this player leaves the table, he gives the dealer the roulette chips, and the dealer gives him $5 in casino chips for each one. Then the color is ready to go again to a new player, and perhaps for a new value.

20. A. Roulette chips are not redeemable at the cashier's cage. You can see why from answer number 19. A player takes a light blue chip to the cashier. The cashier doesn't know how much that chip was worth at the table. It could have been my 25 cents, the next player's $5 or a totally different value from another player.

The cashier will direct the player back to the roulette table where he bought the chip. If the dealer remembers the player and his chip value, and if the pit boss is feeling kind, the roulette chips might be redeemed for full value in casino chips at the table. If too long a time has passed, or the player is not remembered, the player might have to settle for the roulette chips being redeemed for the table minimum.

This all makes sense. With the same chips used as several different denominations per day, neither the cage nor the table crew can be expected to keep track of the chip value for players after they leave the table. Nevertheless, players do sometimes neglect to cash in their chips. A newspaper colleague of mine once wrote a column about a trip to Atlantic City, during which he showed a friend an old trick to make sure he always had money at the end of the trip for cab fare to the airport. He dropped a couple of chips in his pocket, to be forgotten about until checkout day. Unfortunately, the chips he set aside were roulette chips, and when he tried to cash them in it was far too late to get his full value. He got table minimum instead.

Roulette
Spin Number 2:
The Match Game

How much do you win on each winning roulette bet? Do you know the difference between a "street" and a "corner?" And should you find yourself at a single-zero roulette wheel, whether in Monte Carlo, London or Las Vegas, can you say it in French? (Well, in Las Vegas the English names will do.) Try these two matching quizzes. Match up the bet with its payouts. Then match the English bet names with their French equivalents.

Match the bet with its payout.
1. Red or black. (Also odd or even, first 18 or last 18.) ....A. 6-1
2. Dozens (Also 12-number columns.) ....B. 17-1
3. One number. ....C. 1-1
4. Two numbers. ....D. 5-1
5. Three numbers. ....E. 8-1
6. Four numbers. ....F. 35-1
7. Five numbers. ....G. 11-1
8. Six numbers. ....H. 2-1

Most U.S. players know a "split" is a two-number bet; a "street" is a bet on three numbers; a "corner" covers four numbers; and a "double street" is a six-number bet. Every bet also has a French name.

Match the bet with its French equivalent.
1. Red ....A. Carre
2. Black. ....B. Sixaine.
3. Odd ....C. Passe.
4. Even...D. En plein.
5. High ....E. Colonne.
6. Low..F. Pair.
7. Single number ....G. Rouge
8. Split...H. Douzaine
9. Street ....I. Impair
10. Corner ....J. A cheval
11. First four ....K. Noir
12. Double street ....L. Manque
13. Dozen ....M. Transversale
14. Column...N. Quatre premiere

Bonus: Give the French terms for first dozen, middle dozen and last dozen, and first column, middle column and last column.

Roulette
Spin Number 2:
The Match Game
Answers

Match the bet with its payout.

1. C. Red/black, odd/even and first 18/ last 18 all pay 1-1. Make any of them by placing a chip or chips in the rectangle marked for the bet of your choice outside the number layout.

2. H. Dozens (1 through 12, 13 through 24 and 25 through 36) and 12-number columns pay 2-1. You'll find the dozens rectangles on the side of the table near the red/black, odd/even and first 18/last 18 bets. The betting boxes for columns are at the bottom of each column of numbers on the numbers layout.

3. F. One number pays 35-1. Bet on a single number by placing your chip or chips fully within the box containing that number.

4. B. Two numbers pay 17-1. Place a two-number bet by straddling your chip or chip on the line separating your two numbers.

5. G. Three numbers pay 11-1. Place your chip or chips on the line at the left of a row of three consecutive numbers.

6. E. Four numbers pay 8-1. Place your chip or chips at the intersection of four numbers that form a square on the betting layout.

7. A. Five numbers pay 6-1. Place your chip or chips at the border of the layout, straddling the line that separates 0 and 00 from the row of 1, 2 and 3. This is the only five-number bet on the layout, and it exists only in a double-zero game. There is no five-number bet in European roulette.

8. D. Six numbers pay 5-1, and you make the bet by playing your chip or chips so that it straddles the line separating two rows of three at their outer border.

Match the bet with its French equivalent.

1. **G.** Red = Rouge.
2. **K.** Black = Noir
3. **I.** Odd = Impair
4. **F.** Even = Pair.
5. **C.** High (19-36) = Passe.
6. **L.** Low (1-17) = Manque.
7. **D.** Single number = En plein.
8. **J.** Split = Á cheval.
9. **M.** Street = Transversale.
10. **A.** Corner = Carre.
11. **N.** First four = Quatre premiere (0-1-2-3 on single-zero wheel.)
12. **B.** Double street = Sixaine.
13. **H.** Dozen = Douzaine.
14. **E.** Column = Colonne.

Bonus answer: In order, first dozen, middle dozen and last dozen are premiere douzaine, mayenne douzaine and derniere douzaine; first column, middle column and last column are premiere colonne, mayenne colonne and derniere colonne.

Roulette
Spin Number 3:
Bets and Percentages

Knowing the basics of the wagers that can be made and what they pay is a good beginning, but can you apply that knowledge and give yourself a shot to win at roulette? See if you can weed out the true statements about roulette from the false ones.

1. **The house has a higher edge on American roulette than at most table games.**

   True
   False

2. **Roulette moves more slowly than most table games.**

   True
   False

3. **The average player loses no more money per hour at roulette than at other table games.**

   True
   False

4. **Bets on the numbers themselves, whether single-number bets, or two number or any combination, are called "outside bets."**

   True
   False

5. Bets on columns, dozens, evens or odds, reds or blacks are called "outside bets."

   True
   False

6. The player may meet the table minimum bet by combining inside and outside bets.

   True
   False

7. On the inside, the player may spread his minimum bet across several wagers: for example, at a $5 minimum table, he may bet $1 on 17, $1 on 36, split $2 across 0 and 00 and bet $1 on the double street of 4-5-6-7-8-9.

   True
   False

8. On the outside, the player may spread his minimum bet across several wagers: for example, at a $5 minimum table he may bet $1 on red, $1 on the first column, $1 on the first dozen, $1 on odd and $1 on low.

   True
   False

9. For the sake of outside bets, single-zero is considered a black number, while double-zero is red.

   True
   False

10. For the sake of outside bets, single-zero is considered an even number, while double-zero is odd.

    True
    False

11. The house edge at roulette is a result of the presence of zero and double-zero.

True
False

12. **The player can overcome the house edge by placing a split bet on zero and double-zero along with his other wagers.**

   True
   False

13. **The most frequently placed single-number wager is on 17.**

   True
   False

14. **Riverboat casinos frequently add a triple-zero to roulette wheels.**

   True
   False

15. **Each zero added to a wheel gives the house a bigger advantage.**

   True
   False

16. **Roulette is the worst bet in the casino.**

   True
   False

17. **In the United States, roulette players may wager as little as 10 cents on a single number.**

   True
   False

18. **When offered in the United States, single-zero roulette is the same game offered in Europe.**

   True
   False

19. **The worst bet at an American roulette wheel is the five-number combination on 0, 00, 1, 2 and 3.**

True
False

20. The house edge on single-number bets is higher than on even-money bets such as red/black or even/odd.

True
False

Roulette Spin Number 3: Bets and Percentages Answers

1. True. The house edge on most bets at American roulette is 5.26 percent. On the average, for every $100 wagered, the casino is going to keep $5.26. That's considerably higher than the 0.5 percent edge a blackjack basic strategy player faces, or even the 2 to 2.5 percent house edge against an average blackjack player. If craps players stick to the best bets—pass, don't pass, come and don't come—the house edge is only about 1.4 percent, and that can be diluted to 0.8 percent by combining the bets with free odds, which are paid at true odds, or 0.6 percent with double odds. There are worse bets at the craps table, with some propositions having house edges up to 16.67 percent. At baccarat, the house edge is only 1.17 percent on banker and 1.36 percent on player. Caribbean Stud Poker, with a house edge of 5.22 percent of the ante, is closer to the house edge on roulette.

2. True. Whereas blackjack moves at about 50 hands per hour at a full table and more than 200 hands per hour at an empty one, and craps supervisors are looking for more than 100 rolls per hour, roulette is a more majestically paced game. It can move at 65 spins per hour or more with few players, but at a full table with a dealer giving everyone time to get their bets down, it can drop to 30 spins per hour. European games have been known to drop to as few as 10 or 15 spins per hour, but American dealers usually keep the game moving faster.

3. False. The slower pace of the game does make up for

some of the difference in house edge, but it doesn't overcome it entirely.

Let's take an average blackjack player, playing $5 a hand for 50 hands per hour. He risks $250 in an hour. If he loses 2 percent of that, it's a loss of $5. Now let's take a roulette player, also risking $5 per spin. It doesn't matter what the bets are—all but one have the same house edge of 5.26 percent (see answer number 19 in this section). We have a full table, and a cordial dealer making sure everyone has enough time to get their bets down. The game moves at 30 spins per hour, and our player risks $150 per hour—$100 less than at blackjack. But the 5.26 percent house edge means his average losses are $7.89, more than half again his losses at blackjack. Roulette is fun and easy, but the player pays for his entertainment.

4. False. The bets on the numbers—single numbers, splits, streets, corners, five-number and double streets—are inside bets.

5. False. The propositions outside the number layout are the outside bets.

6. False. Inside bets and outside bets must meet the table minimum separately. See answers 7 and 8.

7. True. The player may spread his table minimum bet across several inside wagers. Let's say you're at a table with $5 minimum bets, and you're playing with $1 chips. You meet the $5 minimum if you bet $1 on number 17, $1 on number 36, split $2 between 0 and 00, and bet a $1 double street on 4-5-6-7-8-9.

However, you do not meet the minimum by playing the $1 single number, $1 corner, $1 double street and $2 on red. That bet on red does not count toward your inside total. If you're betting inside, your inside bets must total at least $5.

8. False. Each individual outside wager must at least equal the table minimum. At our $5 table, you cannot reach the table minimum by betting $1 on red, $1 on the first column, $1 on the first dozen, $1 on odd and $1 on low. Your red bet must be at least $5, and if you also want to bet on the first column, that wager also must be at least $5, and so must any other outside bet you make.

9. False. Zero and double zero are neither red nor black. Their background is green both on the wheel and on the table layout. All red bets and all black bets lose if the ball lands in 0 or 00.

10. False. Zero and double zero are neither even nor odd. All even bets and all odd bets lose if the ball lands in 0 or 00.

11. True. The house pays all bets according to odds that would be accurate if there were 36 numbers on the wheel. But with 0 and 00, there are 38 numbers.

To see how this works, let's imagine a perfect series of 38 spins in which the ball lands in each number once. Let's say you're betting $1 on each spin on 29. With 38 spins, you risk a total of $38. On the one spin that the ball lands on 29, you keep your $1 bet and pick up $35 in winnings. You lose $1 on each of the other 37 spins. So at the end of 38 spins, you have $36. The house has won $2 from you. Divide that $2 by your $38 in total wagers, and you have the house edge—5.26 percent.

We can try the same thing with any other bet on the wheel. Let's say you bet $1 on black on each spin. There are 18 black numbers, so on the 18 spins black comes up, you keep your $1 wager and win $1. On the other 20 spins, you lose. At the end of our 38 spins, you have $18 in winnings plus $18 in wagers you didn't lose, a total of $36. The house has $2. Divide that $2 by $38 in total wagers, and you get 0.0526. Multiply by 100 to convert to percent, and you have a house edge of 5.26 percent.

In the real world, there's no such thing as a perfect sequence in which each number comes up once in 38 tries. Sometimes your single number is going to come up twice, even three times in 38 spins. Sometimes black will come up 25 times instead of 18. On those occasions, you'll win. But sometimes your single number won't come up at all, or black will come up only 11 times. Then you'll lose at a rate faster than expected. With millions of customers and billions of wagers, everything balances out for the casino—the house wins 5.26 percent of the money wagered.

12. False. The house edge applies to 0 and 00 just as it does to any other bet on the wheel. And the effect of the house edge is cumulative. If in our perfect sequence of 38 spins we bet $5 on 29 and tried to mitigate the effect of the house edge by also betting a $1 split on 0 and 00, your average losses would be the same as if we'd bet $6 per spin on 29.

On 38 spins at $5 per spin, we'd risk $190. The one time the ball landed in 29, we'd keep our $5 bet and collect $175 in winnings, for a total of $190. So for the 38-spin sequence, we'd lose $10. On the $1 split bet, we'd risk $38. The one time 0 showed up, we'd keep our $1 bet and collect $17 in winnings. Same thing the one time the ball landed in 00: we'd keep our $1 bet and collect $17. After 38 spins, we'd have $36 left for net losses of $2. That makes our overall loss for the sequence $12, with $10 lost on our $5 bets on 29, and $2 lost on our $1 split bets on 0 and 00. We've risked $228 with $190 on 29 and $38 on the split of 0 and 00. We have $216 left—$180 for our one win on 29 and $36 for the two times our split bet won. The house edge for the combination? Divide the $12 in losses by the $228 risked, and you get 0.0526—the same 5.26 house edge as on almost every individual bet on the wheel.

Now let's say we bet $6 per spin on 29 instead. In 38 spins, we risk $228. The one time the ball lands in 29, we keep our $6 and collect $210 in winnings for a total of $216. Our net losses for the sequence amount to $12—the $228 wagered minus the $216 we have left. That's the same $12 total as when we were dividing the bet between 29 and the split on 0 and 00.

13. True. James Bond bets on 17 in the movies, and some Bond fans imitate his bets in the casino. If only we could all win as often as Agent 007.

14. False. The double-zero wheel common in the rest of the United States is also the standard on American riverboat casinos.

15. True. I've mentioned earlier that the single-zero European wheel gives the player a better run for his money than the American double-zero wheel. Here's why: back in number 11, we saw that the house edge comes from the zeroes. On a double-zero wheel, there are 38 numbers, including 0 and 00, and the odds against any number hitting are 37-1. The house pays winning single-number bets at 35-1. Bet $1 on 29 in a perfect sequence of 38 numbers, and you risk $38. You have $36 left, and the house edge is your $2 in losses divided by $38 risked. Multiply by 100 to get percent, and the house edge is 5.26 percent.

On a single-zero wheel, there are only 37 numbers—1 through 36 plus 0. A winning single-number bet still pays 35-1, but our perfect sequence is only 37 numbers long. We risk $37 and get back $36. Now the house edge is $1 in net losses divided by $37 risked, which when converted is 2.7 percent. That works for red/black, even/odd, columns, dozens, corners, streets. On a single-zero wheel, the house edge is 2.7 percent, a little more than half that on a double-zero wheel.

You won't see this in major casinos, but there have been triple-zero wheels. At fairs in Mexico, operators sometimes have used wheels with extra symbols of donkeys or cacti—each special symbol acting like a zero in that any other bet loses when that symbol turns up. Each 0 or special symbol adds to the house edge. With a triple zero, the edge goes up to 7.69 percent; with a fourth zero or special symbol, it's up to 10 percent.

16. False. Some craps bets are truly hideous. A bet on any 7 that pays 4-1 carries a house edge of 16.67 percent. A typical Big Six or money wheel, with the player betting on whether the wheel will stop on $1, $2, $5, $10 or $20 bills or on a special symbol, has house edges ranging from 11 percent to 24 percent.

17. True. At last look, the Gold Spike casino in downtown Las Vegas still was allowing players to break their buy-ins into 10-cent chips. It's easy to spread chips all over the inside when they cost that little. If you look at smaller casinos, it's not difficult to find tables with $1 or $2 table minimums that allow the player to break their bets down into 25-cent or 50-cent chips. Bigger, busier casinos usually have higher minimums both on bet size and chip denomination.

18. False. American casinos usually don't offer the en prison rule that takes roulette to another level. On the even-money outside bets—red/black, even/odd and high/low—you don't necessarily lose when the 0 hits in a European casino. Instead, your bet is "en prison"—in prison.

Let's say I'm in Monte Carlo and I bet 500 francs on black. The ball lands on 0. Instead of picking up my bet, the dealer lets it stand for another spin. If the ball then lends on 0 or red, I lose. But if it lands on black, I get my bet back. This lowers the house edge to 1.35 percent, and makes it a playable game right in line with the best in the casino.

We talked about house edges in answer 1 in this section—0.5 percent against a blackjack basic strategy player, 2 to 2.5 percent an average blackjack player, 1.4 percent on pass/don't pass or come/don't come in craps, 1.17 percent on banker and 1.36 percent on player in baccarat. With a single-zero wheel and the en prison rule, the house edge on roulette fits in with all the best casino games.

19. True. Almost all bets on a double-zero wheel have a house edge of 5.26 percent. The one that doesn't is the five-number bet on 0, 00, 1, 2 and 3. It's worse. The house edge is 7.89 percent—half again as large as the edge on any other wager. Stay away from the five-number bet.

20. False. Even money bets win more frequently than single-number bets, but the 35-1 payoff on a single number balances that off. The house edge on single-number bets and even-money bets is the same 5.26 percent on a double-zero wheel.

Roulette
Spin Number 4:
Wagers and Systems

Roulette has been around long enough that mathematicians as well as the betting public have tried over and over to find a flaw that would make the game vulnerable to systems play. The game is mathematically sound—if all is right in the casino, players shouldn't be able to beat it consistently. Yet sometimes they do. See how much you know about the conditions that can shift the edge away from the house. A caution: don't get your hopes up. Beatable wheels aren't common, and beating them takes a lot of work.

1. **On an American wheel, the house edge on most roulette bets:**

    A. Is the same as on most others.
    B. Goes up as the payout on the bet rises.
    C. Falls as the payout on the bet rises.

2. **A few American casinos, particularly in Atlantic City, lower the house edge with an option called:**

    A. En prison.
    B. Surrender.
    C. Double or nothing.

3. **The worst bet on a European wheel is:**

    A. Four-number.
    B. Five-number.
    C. There isn't one.

4. **Some players try to overcome the house edge by using betting systems instead of trying to identify the numbers most likely to hit. One common system is to double your bet after each loss; when a win eventually comes, you're left with a profit for the sequence. This system is called:**

   A. d'Alembert.
   B. Cancellation.
   C. Martingale.

5. **Given enough time and money on the player's part, the double-up system described above would always work if:**

   A. The casino didn't change dealers.
   B. There were no betting limits.
   C. The wheel was perfectly balanced.

6. **The "cancellation" system involves:**

   A. Cancelling bets after seeing the dealer's release point.
   B. Crossing out numbers in a series with each winning bet until a goal is reached.
   C. Betting 0 and 00 to cancel out the house edge.

7. **The "d'Alembert" system assumes:**

   A. Wins and losses will balance out in the long run.
   B. A perfectly balanced wheel.
   C. Wheel biases favor the player.

8. **Betting red and odd at the same time:**

   A. Means the player will do no worse than break even on a majority of spins.
   B. Decreases the house edge.
   C. Increases the house edge.

9. **Which best describes betting single numbers as opposed to betting an equal amount on red or black?**

   A. Yields bigger losses in the long run.

    B. Yields bigger wins in the long run.

    C. Yields more volatile short-term results.

10. **The house edge on American roulette is comparable to:**

    A. Craps.

    B. $1 slots.

    C. Baccarat.

11. **Many casinos now have electronic boards that display the numbers that have come up on the previous 12 or 18 spins. Most of the time, this posting:**

    A. Helps the player.

    B. Helps the house.

    C. Makes no difference.

12. **If red has come up the last 12 spins in a row, the next spin is:**

    A. More likely than usual to be black.

    B. Less likely than usual to be black.

    C. As likely as usual to be black.

13. **If 17 has come up the last three spins in a row, the next spin is:**

    A. More likely than usual to be 17.

    B. Less likely than usual to be 17.

    C. About as likely as usual to be 17.

14. **If over thousands of spins, some numbers occur more frequently than expected by random chance, the wheel is said to be:**

    A. Biased.

    B. Gaffed.

    C. Crooked.

15. **If some numbers consistently occur more frequently than expected by random chance, this:**

    A. Favors the house.

    B. Favors the player.

    C. Makes no difference.

16. **The player observes that five numbers are landing more frequently than others. Which is more likely to indicate a biased wheel?**

    A. 1-2-3-4-5.

    B. 32-33-34-35-36.

    C. 00-1-10-13-27.

17. **If charting thousands of spins has proven some numbers are occuring more frequently than expected by chance, the best way to proceed is:**

    A. If the majority of frequent numbers are red, bet red; if the majority are black, bet black.

    B. Use three-number streets and four-number corners inside, covering the frequent numbers with as few bets as possible.

    C. Bet single numbers.

18. **Some players watch the dealer to try to predict where the ball will land. They watch for:**

    A. Variations in the dealer's speed.

    B. The release point of the ball.

    C. How quickly the ball falls to the center.

19. **Dealers most likely to be successfully tracked are:**

    A. Just out of dealer's school.

    B. Job-hoppers.

    C. Veterans.

20. **When another player is winning heavily, it might be wise to:**

    A. Bet with that player.

    B. Bet opposite that player, figuring luck is due to change.

    C. Ignore that player.

Roulette
Spin Number 4:
Wagers and Systems
Answers

1. A. Just seeing if you're paying attention. If you've taken a spin through the last quiz, you know the house edge is 5.26 percent on every bet on a double-zero wheel except the five-number bet on 0, 00, 1, 2 and 3. On that combination, the house edge is 7.89 percent.

2. B. Surrender is the American equivalent of the European en prison rule. On even-money bets, when the ball lands on 0 or 00, the player surrenders half his bet. That lowers the house edge on even-money bets to 2.6 percent—not as good as the 1.35 percent on European wheels with en prison (see answer 18 in *Roulette Spin Number 3*), but far better than 5.26 percent. Surrender is not a common rule, but it's worth asking about when you play.

3. C. There is no one bet on the single-zero wheel that has a higher house edge than another as there is with the five-number bet on a double-zero wheel. The house edge on all bets on the European wheel is 2.7 percent, unless en prison is offered. That makes the even-money bets—red/black, even/odd, high/low—better than the rest with a house edge of 1.35 percent. But there still is no one worst bet.

4. C. The betting system in which the player doubles his bet after each loss is called the Martingale.

5. B. The Martingale is a very old system, and sooner or later nearly every player ponders giving it a try on the even-money bets.

In theory, if you always doubled your bet after a loss, when you eventually won you'd be left with a profit equal to your original bet. This works in a short sequence. If you start with a $5 bet and lose, your next bet is $10. If you win the $10 bet, you have a $5 profit for the sequence. If you lose, you bet $20—enough to give you a $5 profit if you win. The problem is that you quickly get into large numbers. Starting with $5, a 10-step Martingale takes you to bets of $10, $20, $40, $80, $160, $320, $640, $1,280 and $2,560. I don't know about you, but I'd be more than a little queasy putting $2,560 on the line in hopes of salvaging a $5 profit for the sequence.

Even if you were of a mind to do such a thing, the casino won't let you. That's why there are maximum bets at each table. A $5 minimum table might have maximum bet of $500. I've seen as low as $100 and as high as $2,000, but $500 is pretty typical. With a $500 maximum, your Martingale is finished at seven steps. If you lose your seventh bet of $320, the most you can wager is $500. You can no longer make a bet that will give you a profit for the sequence.

Gamblers underestimate just how often a sequence as long as seven losses in a row happens. If you were flipping a coin, a 50-50 proposition, the chances that heads will come up seven times in a row are 1 in 128. If you played a seven-step Martingale on each sequence, starting with a $5 bet and doubling after each loss until maxing out at a $320 bet to stay under the table maximum, you would win $5 on each of 127 sequences, for a total of $635 in winnings. On the one seven-loss sequence, you would lose your $320 big bet, plus bets of $160, $80, $40, $20, $10 and $5. That's a total of $635 in losses—a wash. You break even, as you should in the long run when flipping a coin.

But the roulette even-money bets are not the same as flipping the coin. You don't have a 50 percent chance of winning when you bet on black; you have a 47.37 percent chance. That means your seven-loss sequence isn't a 1-in-128 shot; it'll happen about once per 90 sequences. Start with $5 on black in a seven-step Martingale, and you'll win your $5 89 of 90 times for $445 in winnings. But on the one losing sequence, you lose $635 and wonder why you ever convinced yourself this was a good idea.

6. B. In a cancellation system, the player starts by writing a series of numbers, and the total is his win goal for the sequence. Let's take a three-number cancellation—1, 1, 1. The win goal for the sequence is three units, or, for a $5 bettor, $15. Each bet will be the sum of the numbers on each end. Here, the starting point is two units, $10. If the bet wins, the bettor crosses off, or cancels, the number on each end, then bets the sum of the new end numbers. In this case, if the first bet won, the second bet would be the remaining number, one unit, or $5.

If the first bet loses, the player writes the number of units bet at the end of the sequence. Here he's left with a new sequence of 1, 1, 1, 2. The next bet becomes the sum of the new end numbers—three units, or $15. If he loses again, he writes records that three-unit bet at the end of his sequence, which now stretches to 1, 1, 1, 2, 3. The next bet is four units—the sum of the numbers on each end—or, for a $5 player, $20. When the player wins enough bets that all numbers have been crossed off, the player has reached his win goal.

You can see the problem here. With a few losses, the sequences stretches and becomes unwieldy, and the losses mount. The bets do not quickly reach the astronomical range of the Martingale. However, neither does a single winning bet end the sequence. One big losing sequence eats of the profits of many smaller wins.

7. A. In the d'Alembert system, the player assumes that after a win, he is less likely to win again. Therefore, he subtracts a chip from his bet. After a loss, he figures a win is more likely than another loss, so he adds a chip to his bet.

The foremost problem here is that the wheel doesn't know it's supposed to balance things out. The wheel has no memory, and it doesn't know whether the last spin was red or black, even or odd. The chances of any spin coming up with a red number are 18 in 38. That remains 18 in 38 even if the last spin, or the last 10, or the last 100 also were red. The outcome of the previous bet has no effect on the likely outcome of the next bet.

8. A. A couple of years ago I was speaking at the same convention as were several other authors of gambling books. One recommended that roulette players combine a red/black bet with an odd/even bet. That way, he said, they'd have three-quarters of the numbers covered. Some of the numbers would be covered twice, and those numbers could enable the player to squeeze out a nice profit.

There are problems with this, however. Let's use red and even, because 10 of the 18 black numbers are even. We actually cover 28 numbers this way—the 18 red numbers plus the black even numbers 2, 4, 6, 8, 10, 20, 22, 24, 26 and 28. That's not quite three quarters of the numbers including 0 and 00—75 percent of 38 is 28.5—but there's no need to be pedantic.

Let's go back to our perfect sequence of 38 spins in which each number comes up once. On each spin, we bet $5 on red and $5 on even. That's a total of $10 per spin and $380 for our sequence. We do actually collect money on 28 of the 38 spins. However, whenever any of the black even numbers win, the bet on red loses, so we just break even for the spin. Similarly, whenever the red odd numbers hit—1, 3, 5, 7, 9, 19, 21, 23, 25 or 27—we win on red and lose on even, breaking even for the spin.

The good spins for us are when any of the red even numbers hit. If the ball falls in 12, 14, 16, 18, 30, 32, 34 or 36, we win both on red and even. Those are the ones we're hoping for. The black odd numbers along with 0 and 00 are bad spins for us. We lose both bets when those numbers hit. So we have four possibilities:

- On red even numbers we win both on red and even, keeping our $10 in wagers and making $10 in profit each time. There are eight of these numbers, so these eight wins give us $160.
- On red odd numbers we win on red but lose on even. We break even, keeping $10 for each of those 10 numbers. That gives us $100 on these spins.

- On black even numbers we win on even but lose on red. We break even for each of 10 spins, meaning we keep another $100.
- On black odd numbers, 0 and 00, we lose both on red and even. There are eight black odd numbers, and 0 and 00 bring the number of total loss spins up to 10.

Add up the $160 we have on red even numbers to the $100 on red odds and the $100 on black evens, and at the end of the 38-spin sequence we have $360 of our original $380. The house has $20, and if you've been paying attention I'll bet you can tell me what percent of our wagers that is without doing the arithmetic. Yep, it's 5.26 percent, the same as the house edge on almost every bet on the table.

Combination bets can't overcome the house edge. That doesn't mean they're worthless. Playing a combination like this decreases the likelihood you'll go broke in just a few spins. If you're looking to play for a long time and have some fun, this way will keep you in action a lot longer than playing single numbers. You're trading off the chance of bigger instant profits if your single number shows up an extra time or two for the stability of having a lot of numbers working.

9. C. In the long run, the house is going to take the same percentage out of single-number bets that it does out of red/black bets. The short-term results are more volatile with single-number bets, however.

Let's say you stay long enough for 38 spins of the wheel. If you're playing $5 on the same single number each time, the most likely result is that it'll come up once, and you'll be a $10 loser for the session. But it could come up twice, making you a $170 winner for the session, or it could come up not at all, making you a $190 loser. All that is well within the range of normal chance.

If you're betting black, the most likely result is that black will come up 18 times, and you'll be a $10 winner for the session. Chances are minuscule that it would come up 36 times, giving you the same $170 profit as a single number hitting twice. And chances are microscopic that black would not come up at all, making you a $190 loser.

By having 18 numbers working at once, you take away the extremes. You're unlikely to be a big winner, and you're unlikely to be a big loser. Chances are you'll wind up somewhere between a $30 loser and a $20 winner.

10. B. Depending on where in the country you're playing, $1 slots return about 94 percent to 96 percent of all coins played. That's the equivalent of a house edge of 4 percent to 6 percent.

However, despite the similar house edges, $1 slot machines eat up the cash far faster than roulette. Modern slots with currency acceptors enable players to play off credits rather than feed in coins for every pull. Steady players easily can get in 500 pulls per hour, and some players go far faster. Playing two credits at a time, the $1 slot player risks $1,000 per hour, for average hourly losses of $40 to $60. That dwarfs the expected $7.89 average hourly loss for a $5 roulette player.

11. C. Twelve-to-eighteen spins is far too short a time to determine whether there's a pattern of numbers hitting more often than expected by random chance. Four thousand spins would be more like it. But there is no harm in playing numbers that have come up more than once in the last several spins. At worst, you're playing against the same 5.26 percent edge as on any other number. At best, you might just be lucking into a non-random wheel.

12. C. Any red/black pattern that shows on the electronic board is just random chance. Even after charting thousands of spins, any analysis that finds a pattern is going to find individual numbers that come more often than they should, not a bias toward red or black.

13. C. Twelve-to-eighteen spins is nowhere near a statistically significant sample, and a number hitting three times in a row is probably just random chance. Still, I'd be tempted to put a few chips on 17 as well as 5 and 32—the numbers on either side of 17 on the wheel.

14. A. We like biased wheels, especially when we know they're biased. We dream of taking advantage of such things and making lots of money. We don't want to encounter gaffed or crooked wheels, which can be manipulated to fleece the customers. We trust state gaming authorities to keep such things out of modern casinos.

15. B. If some numbers occur more often than by random chance, and the player knows about it, it favors the player. The house does not want a biased wheel. If all numbers come up as expected by random chance, the house edge keeps the profits coming in. A biased wheel opens the door for smart players to clean up.

16. C. That sequence, 00-1-10-13-27, is made up of five consecutive numbers on the wheel. If those five numbers are hitting more often that expected by chance, we can be pretty sure there's a bias in that section of the wheel. The sequences listed in A. and B. are consecutive numbers on the table layout. The numbers are not in numerical on the wheel. A bias toward numbers in numerical order as opposed to wheel order is highly improbable.

17. C. If you've discovered a wheel bias, you want to maximize your profit opportunity. Betting single numbers is the way to go. If you've put in the work of charting and analyzing numbers for days on end, and finally uncovered a wheel bias, you're not going to want to waste your knowledge on low-paying wagers.

18. B. The feeling is that some dealers get in a rut, and that they spin the wheel and release the ball with about the same velocity every time. That gives their spins a trackable signature. If the player can judge the dealer's release point relative to the wheel, and he knows that with this dealer the ball often lands about the same distance around the wheel from the release point, he can bet accordingly.

19. C. Veteran dealers who have been in the same routine for decades are believed to be the most likely to fall into the routine of releasing the ball the same way every spin.

20. A. You're probably just encountering a player on a lucky streak, but there's an outside shot you're seeing a player who knows something instead. Maybe they've spotted a wheel bias or a dealer tendency. Most likely, they're just lucky, but there's no harm in playing with the hot hand.

Bibliography

When I search for the answers to my casino questions, I've found many publications invaluable. These are some of the best I've found:

BOOKS ON BLACKJACK

Best Blackjack by Frank Scoblete, Bonus Books, 160 East Illinois Street, Chicago, IL 60611. $14.95.

Beat the Dealer by Edward O. Thorp, Vintage Books, 201 East 50th Street, New York, NY 10022. $7.95.

The Theory of Blackjack by Peter Griffin, Huntington Press, 3687 South Procyon Avenue, Las Vegas, NV 89103. $11.95.

Basic Blackjack ($14.95) and *Professional Blackjack* ($19.95) by Stanford Wong, Pi Yee Press, 7910 Ivanhoe Avenue, #34, La Jolla, CA 92037.

Blackjack Bluebook by Fred Renzey, *The Blackjack Mentor*, P.O. Box 598, Elk Grove, IL 60009. $12.95.

The World's Greatest Blackjack Book by Lance Humble and Carl Cooper, Doubleday, 566 5th Avenue, New York, NY 10103. ($9.95.)

Blackbelt in Blackjack by Arnold Snyder, RGE Publishing, 414 Santa Clara Avenue, Oakland, CA 94610 ($12.95).

Blackjack: Take the Money and Run by Henry J. Tamburin, Research Services Unlimited, 6920 Airport Boulevard, #117-111, Mobile, AL 36608. $11.95.

Million Dollar Blackjack by Ken Uston, Gambling Times/ Carol Publishing Group, 600 Madison Avenue, New York, NY 10022. $16.95.

The Ultimate Blackjack Book by Walter Thomason, Carole Publishing, 600 Madison Avenue, New York, NY 10022. $14.95.

BOOKS ON VIDEO POKER

America's Naiional Game of Chance: Video Poker ($19.95) and *Winning Strategies for Video Poker* ($15.95) by Lenny Frome, Compu-Flyers, 5025 S. Eastern Avenue, Las Vegas, NV 89119.

Victory at Video Poker by Frank Scoblete, Bonus Books, 160 East Illinois Street, Chicago, IL 60611. $12.95.

Video Poker Precision Play ($12.95) *and The Best of Video Poker Times* ($24.95) by Dan Paymar, published by Dan Paymar, 2540 S. Maryland Parkway, Suite 141, Las Vegas, NV 89109.

Video Poker Mania by Dwight Crevelt and Louise Crevelt, Gollehon Press, Grand Rapids, MI. $4.95.

BOOKS ON ROULETTE

Beating the Wheel by Russell T. Barnhart, Carol Publishing, 600 Madison Avenue, New York, NY 10022. $12.95.

The Eudaemonic Pie by Thomas A. Bass, Vintage Books, 201 East 50th Street, New York, NY. $5.95.

Spin Roulette Gold by Frank Scoblete, Bonus Books, 160 East Illinois Street, Chicago, IL 60611. $14.95.

GENERAL GAMING GUIDES

The Experts' Guide to Casino Games, edited by Walter Thomason, Carol Publishing, 600 Madison Avenue, New York, NY 10022. $16.95.

Smart Casino Gambling by Olaf Vancura, Index Publishing Group, 3368 Governor Drive, Suite 273, San Diego, CA, 92122 ($24.95).

Scarne's New Complete Guide to Gambling by John Scarne,

Fireside Books, Simon and Schuster Building, Rockefeller Center, 1230 Avenue of the Americas, New York, NY 10020. $17.95.

NEWSLETTERS

Frank Scoblete's *Chance and Circumstance*, published quarterly by Paone Press, P.O. Box 610, Lynbrook, NY 11563. $40 for one year, single issue $11.95. Includes articles by Scoblete, Alene Paone, John Robison, Henry Tamburin, Walter Thomason and John Grochowski.

Anthony Curtis' *Las Vegas Advisor,* published monthly by Huntington Press, 3687 South Procyon Avenue, Las Vegas, NV 89103. $50 for one year; single issue $5. If you want to get the most out of Las Vegas, from gambling to dining to entertainment, this is your guide.

OTHER BOOKS BY JOHN GROCHOWSKI

Gaming: Cruising the Casinos with Syndicated Gambling Columnist John Grochowski, Running Count Press, P.O. Box 1488, Elmhurst IL 60126, or call Huntington Press at (800) 244-2224. $11.95. A compilation of 67 essays on casino gambling, from blackjack to baccarat and slot clubs to progressive betting.

Winning Tips for Casino Games, Publications International, 7373 N. Cicero Avenue, Lincolnwood, IL 60646. $4.99. This 144-page small format paperback is a basic primer on how to play casino games.

The Experts' Guide to Casino Games, edited by Walter Thomason, Carol Publishing, 600 Madison Avenue, New York, NY 10022. $16.95. John is one of eight co-authors, having provided a brief history of gaming in the United States and a chapter on blackjack. Other co-authors are Frank Scoblete, Henry Tamburin, Walter Thomason, Alene Paone, Steve Bourie, Jim Hildebrand and John Rainey.